ADULT LEARNING
ADULT TEACHING

ADULT LEARNING
ADULT TEACHING

Fourth Edition

John Daines
with
Carolyn Daines and Brian Graham

Welsh Academic Press

Published in Wales by Welsh Academic Press, an imprint of

Ashley Drake Publishing Ltd
PO Box 733
Cardiff
CF14 7ZY
www.ashleydrake.com

First published by the University of Nottingham,
Department of Continuing Education 1988
Reprinted 1990, 1991
Second Edition published 1992
Reprinted with minor amendments 1993
Third Edition published 1993
Reprinted 1994, 1995, 1996, 1997, 1998

Published by Welsh Academic Press 2002
Reprinted 2004
Fourth Edition Published 2006

ISBN 1 86057 115 8

British Library Cataloguing-in-Publication Data
A CIP catalogue for this book is available from the British Library.

Printed by Gutenberg Press, Malta

Contents

Preface

This book is intended to provide some practical suggestions for all those involved in teaching and working with adults. It is concerned with the ways that adults learn and how tutors and trainers can help them learn more efficiently. Most of the book is based upon what we have learned over a number of years of teaching adults and running training courses for adult education tutors, for tutor trainers and for other professional groups who increasingly find themselves in the business of adult learning and teaching. We usually work by applying our experience to what we plan and do rather than deducing it from theory, and this is what we have tried to do in this book too.

This fourth edition has been completely rewritten, updated and contains several totally new chapters. We have again tried to provide an accessible and practical account of how to set about the effective planning, preparation and teaching of courses for adults.

There are two major parts to the book. The first is concerned with adult learning – adults as learners, their characteristics, expectations, and so on. One of the new chapters – 'The pottery class: a student's experience' – is a forthright account of what goes on in the classroom as seen from a learner's perspective. We have added some critical feedback addressed to her tutor.

The second part is concerned with adult teaching, and has sections on planning for learning, methods, and reviewing learning. With the increased importance being given to the quality assurance of educational provision for adults, we have included a chapter about class visits and 'Observing teaching and learning'.

The fourth and final section is about getting started and looks at the sharp end, not least of which is in 'Self presentation' and 'Difficult students'!

We are most grateful to Sue Butler and Dr Bob Chapman for their assistance and we hope that the ideas and suggestions included here will confirm you in what you are already doing well, and help you to develop your practice to the benefit of the adults you work with.

Enjoy your teaching.

John Daines, Carolyn Daines and Brian Graham

ADULT LEARNING

Until relatively recently, it was generally thought that adults acquired new knowledge and skills in much the same way as they did when they were children. However, as we discover more about the way that the brain works and investigate more closely what younger people and adults actually do, this seems less sure. Whilst it is unlikely that adult learning differs qualitatively as well as quantitatively from that of children across the board, there are areas of divergence. Children pass through cognitive developmental stages. At one time, it was thought that this ceased at adolescence, though it now seems likely that this continues into adulthood too. The brain appears to be 'under construction' until well into the twenties. People develop preferences in the ways they approach learning and in the formats in which material is encountered, though the underlying process of learning – acquisition, storage and retrieval – remains much the same. There are subtle changes in memory performance as adults get older and there are differences in interest and in motivation too. But whatever the variation in cognitive processes may be, there is no doubt that compared with children, adults bring a massive amount of acquired knowledge, skills, understanding and experience to all that they do. Much of this learning has been via problem solving, discovery, informal mentoring and social interaction, rather than in a classroom or with the help of a professional tutor. All in all, they possess considerable stores of wisdom which they are able to apply to life, and they can make informed choices that are cognitively and emotionally much more advanced than those made by young people.

As teachers of adults we need to take account of the ways adults learn and their expectations and motives for engaging in the more formalised learning activities through which we meet them. The next few pages consider some of the important features.

I Adults as Learners

1 Learning in Adulthood

Rather than describe the psychology of conditioning and learning or give details of adult learning theory, we have drawn together some of the key points from a present understanding of the process of adult learning which have implications for the teachers of adults.

1 Given freedom from disease, injury or abuse, the human brain can and does remain fully functioning throughout life. We do not arrive at a mental plateau as we reach biological maturity; we do not fall into cognitive decline, nor is the potential for new learning lost. The adage 'you can't teach an old dog new tricks' is quite misleading since as people get older they so obviously can and do go on learning.

2 Whilst some physical capabilities do deteriorate with age – sensory acuity, strength and stamina – it seems unlikely that overall physiological decline has any significant effect on adult learning potential. There are, nevertheless, some age related decrements, not least a tendency to temporarily forget names of things and people, and to under-perform tasks that demand speed as well as accuracy.

3 Learning is the cognitive mechanism by which we process information, resulting in relatively permanent change in response potential. It is the means by which we gain and retain our impressions of the world and our place within it, whether the learning is being consciously undertaken through education and training, or occurring below the level of consciousness in day to day living. It can involve changes in knowledge, skills, emotions, values and attitudes.

4   Learning is concerned with the acquisition, storage and retrieval of material – more commonly thought of as learning, memory and remembering (whether by recall or recognition). Forgetting is a failure to retrieve, either because of some cognitive or emotional interference, or because the material was poorly acquired in the first place.
   When information from the senses reaches the brain, a variety of transformations take place. Decisions are made as to whether the incoming data is important, whether it matches existing knowledge and understanding, and the need to create new associations and their 'laying down' as stored (and potentially retrievable) neural memory pathways. Some time ago, Broadbent[1] offered a helpful analogy which likens this Information Processing model of learning and memory to the ways in which a librarian functions within a library. As the information – a book – comes in, it is actively stored. This requires an individual to analyse and perhaps transform the information, to make reference to what is already known – held on the shelves – and then to label it in a variety of ways – index reference system – that will allow it to be subsequently located and used.

5   Learning is influenced by the personal relevance that new material has for us, its similarity to what we may already know, and to our level of interest in it. Brain mechanisms interpret the new material, compare it with existing knowledge and actively synthesise new links and associations. Thus, it is easier to learn something new about a known topic or to enhance a set of existing skills than it is to deal with a totally novel concept or acquire a completely new technique. On occasion, new material can conflict with what is already known. Existing knowledge and understanding can interfere with new ideas or ways of doing something and prevent them from being properly learnt. Learning is also influenced by our physical and emotional states as well as by our levels of motivation, anxieties about potential or imagined failure, stress, emotional blocks and lack of self-confidence.

[1] Broadbent, DA *Cognitive Psychology and Education*. B. J. Ed. Psychol., 1975, 45, 2, 162–176.

6   Much of what we daily experience is not permanently stored. We may simply not be attending to something because it seems irrelevant – though this implies that we must have made an active if subconscious analytical judgement about it in order to disregard it. An experience may also lose out to more pressing thoughts and feelings, or an already stored memory fades from lack of use. For the elderly, the past – or at least the memorable and important episodes – can become more personally important than the mundane present.

7   Discovering that an act of learning is useful and rewarding, results in people being more likely to continue with, return to, or repeat a thought process or task. This is true when they perceive ongoing success for themselves as well as when they are given positive feedback by others. When individuals receive reinforcement for a partially successful action, especially when it is coupled with information on how to improve, they are likely to modify the approach and try again with renewed motivation to achieve further success.

KEY POINTS

* *Adults continue to learn throughout life.*
* *The more relevant and comprehensible the original learning, the more permanent and retrievable the material learnt.*

2 Learning Styles

There has been considerable interest shown of late in learning styles. The prominence that the concept has been given suggests that for some educators and agencies, learning styles are *the* crucial feature of the human learning process. Whilst learning styles may well be of importance, they are far from the whole story of how people learn. Moreover, there is a singular lack of agreement about how learning styles can be categorised and how alternative style descriptions articulate one with another, or indeed, whether they can.

1   Within the description of learning and memory offered by the information processing model described above, learning styles are seen to be a contributory influence (or set of influences) upon the learning process and not a discrete entity. Individuals probably do have preferences for the format in which material is initially encountered and for the way(s) in which they manipulate newly acquired information and link it with that which is already stored.

But whatever learning styles actually are, significant caution in their application is presently called for. A recent critical review[2] shows that the concept of learning styles, first suggested by Kolb fifty years ago, is now used by various theorists to encompass more than 30 different preference dichotomies including verbalisers versus imagers, activist vs reflectors, and left brainers vs right brainers. This extensive study of a dozen or so different models has indicated serious design weakness in practically all of them, including low reliability (test/retest consistency) and poor validity (measuring what something says it measures). There is the additional problem that they nearly all rely upon self-report inventories – people's impressions of themselves – rather than objective observation of their actual behaviour.

---

[2] Coffield, F. et al, 2004; *Should we use learning styles?* LSRC, 2004

2   These uncertainties not withstanding, learning style inventories
     are being recommended for widespread use with the intention of
     facilitating learning and teaching through the 'personalisation'
     of learning. Their proponents believe that they can diagnose how
     individuals prefer to learn and, as a result, help them capitalise
     on this self-awareness. There are further expectations that such
     diagnoses will help tutors to modify their teaching methodologies
     to accord with their learners' individual preferences.

     One model – Illustration 1 – refers to the form in which
     information is initially received by the senses and subsequently
     processed during the acquisition stages. It makes use of three
     sensory preferences: visual, aural and touch/handling.

'Visual' learners value	'Auditory' learners value	'Practical' learners value
• seeing things in print • using colour, diagrams and illustrations • seeing things demonstrated • looking at or examining objects • having notes with diagrams	• listening to explanations • talking about ideas and problems • listening to a tape • taping notes and revision • asking questions and hearing answers	• doing hands-on tasks • doing rather thanlistening • manipulating objects • solving practical problems • working 1:1 • helping others

Illustration 1: Learning styles as sensory preferences

Another model refers to individually preferred ways of
handling material – of making connections with pre-existing
knowledge and conceptual understanding – as well as how the
synthesised and stored material is subsequently used 'post
retrieval'. It uses 4 categories – activist, theorist, reflector, and
pragmatist – and completing the model's inventory is said to
provide a profile of stronger and weaker learning preferences.
The left hand column of Illustration 2 (page 8) shows the
behaviours judged to be characteristic of each preference.

3   Some ACL (Adult and Community Learning) providers ask adult students to complete learning styles inventories, to discover their individual styles, to work to their preferences and to recognise/ enhance their less preferred formats. In turn, the tutor will facilitate each individual's learning by choosing methods that play to that learner's diagnosed strengths. Given that any inventory in use *is* valid and reliable (and psychometrically robust and well grounded in verified theory) this appears a desirable objective when part of an overall strategy of differentiating between the needs of individual students, and modifying their teaching and learning opportunities.

4   However, we are not convinced that learning style technology has developed to the point where it should have this determining influence on teaching. You should certainly talk with your students and discover from them their individual likes, dislikes and preferences ... and if a *good* inventory does aid this, use it. However, since one of the main tasks of any tutor is to enhance people's learning and their capacity to learn in a range of ways, you should already be using a variety of methods and approaches to allow everyone to benefit from at least a proportion of them. Thus by design or accident, you will be matching what you do to what they may well prefer, as well as helping them to learn from (apparently) less preferred activities.

5   As an afterthought, the recognition that each tutor may have preferred learning styles and as a consequence, teach in a particular way *is* an arresting thought. If *you* have developed a preferred way(s) of learning and handling new materials *as a learner*, you would need to think about the ways you teach. Critically, are you using activities and methods that suit *your* preferred way(s) of learning rather than those of your students? The right hand column of Illustration 2 indicates the probable teaching behaviours of tutors with particular learning styles preferences and who thus favour their use in teaching. If you are limiting the ways in which you teach to the ways that work for you, you may be disadvantaging a number of those you are trying to help.

Learner preferences	Associated teaching behaviours
'Activist' learners • thrive on new experiences • are very active and enthusiastic • act first and consider consequences later • have a low boredom threshold • are gregarious • are open-minded, not sceptical • are willing to try anything once	**'Activist' tutors** • are active/enthusiastic communicators • deliver action packed sessions • try out new ideas in courses/programmes • seek to provide new experiences • place little emphasis on theory • give little time to reflection before moving • on to the next activity
'Theorist' learners • are logical • are good at analysis and synthesis • are keen on assumptions, principles, theories, models • feel uncomfortable with subjective judgements • prefer to maximise certainty • prize rationality and logic • tend to be perfectionists	**'Theorist' tutors** • are very well grounded in theory • are unlikely to take risks with untested ideas • want to offer proven ideas and methods • emphasise facts and logic • offer well researched/prepared materials • may place emphasis on experiential • learning
'Reflective' learners ... • stand back and ponder • observe from many perspectives • think thoroughly before coming to any conclusion • are cautious • are 'thoughtful' and good listeners • adopt a low profile • can see the bigger picture	**'Reflective' tutors** • have a low key approach • adopt a slower pace to allow people to digest and reflect • play the role of observer • are interested in exploring all angles of the situation • set the course in the wider context
'Pragmatic' learners • enjoy testing ideas/techniques to see if they work in practice • adopt a practical down to earth approach • enjoy making practical decisions and problem solving • become impatient with ruminating/open ended discussions • like to get on with things • think that if it works, it's good	**'Pragmatic' tutors ...** • focus on practical applications, ideas, theories and concepts • discuss new ideas in terms of whether they will work in practice • experiment to test out practical use • avoid theory which has no clear practical relevance

Illustration 2: Learning styles as processing/behavioural preferences

KEY POINTS

- *Find out about people's preferred ways of working, not only their 'learning styles' but also their organisational, feedback and other personal preferences.*
- *Use a wider range of methods and approaches to suit most people more of the time.*

3 Some Characteristics of Adults as Learners

People come to adult education from widely varying backgrounds and at different stages of life, each one an individual with his or her own personal strengths, hopes and anxieties. The tutor's job is to recognise the uniqueness of each person and to work in ways that will best help each individual to achieve his or her objectives. Nevertheless, there are a number of characteristic features that may usefully describe many adult learners.

1 Adults bring to their studies a considerable store of knowledge and experience gained over the years, much of which will be relevant to what is to be learnt. They have the potential to transfer what they already know to their current learning, either directly or by being helped to make the appropriate links.

2 Adults bring their own particular ways of doing things, patterns of thought and attitudes to help them cope with new situations and ideas. At the same time, over-learnt habits and strongly held beliefs can prove disadvantageous where they prevent individuals from considering and learning something new, whether it is a different technique, an alternative set of values, a recent development or a novel idea. They may need convincing that a new way is worth trying.

3 Though adults may not have been directly involved in formal education for some years, they will still have learnt a great deal in the course of their lives since leaving school or college. Their learning, especially of practical things, will not have been drawn from principles and theory, nor involved a great deal of abstract thought. They are much more likely to have handled concrete issues and to have solved practical problems for themselves 'by doing'. Their implicit theory will have been drawn from practice through discovery, trial and error, and proven success, rather than the other way round.

4   Adults, especially the more elderly, may find it difficult to recall isolated facts and to learn under pressure. On the other hand, they have significant powers of comprehension and of organising material into meaningful wholes. It is unusual for adults to have to acquire totally new concepts – a major development task for children. Generally, adults possess a comprehensive mental representation of the world and much adult learning has to do with extending and developing existing conceptual schema. Where these do not exist, new learning may prove a considerable challenge, e.g. aspects of the information technology revolution.

5   Adults can lack confidence in themselves as learners as well as under-estimating their powers and potential. They tend to be over-anxious and are reluctant to risk making mistakes. Above all they will not want to fail or look foolish. These reactions can be particularly prevalent in those who have had poor learning experiences at school. Such negative reactions are also likely to be strongly felt by those who have had experienced inequality, prejudice or have been made to feel different. A sense of anxiety can be a handicap for adult learners, especially where they feel they have to learn in overly competitive or hostile situations.

6   Adults are unlikely to be satisfied with a time perspective that sees learning as a lengthy process in which the attainment of a desired outcome is in the distant future. For many people the value of learning is predominantly in the here and now, rather than long term; indeed the more elderly may perceive time to be running short. Nevertheless, they recognise they will not be able to acquire everything straightaway or necessarily be successful on the first occasion they attempt something. They are likely to be satisfied with a balance – some current success, which can be seen to be building towards an achievable and satisfying goal.

7   The learning commitment of adults is normally part-time. They combine attending a course with family responsibilities and with an occupation, whether they work in the home, in paid employment or in an unwaged capacity. They may not be able to devote much additional time to their studies beyond the

confines of the course, however interested or motivated they are. They may arrive 'next time' with little more achieved than when they left 'last time'.

8   Adults can be expected to have assumed responsibility for themselves. In their private lives at least, they are accustomed to setting their own goals and deciding what they want to do and how they want to do it. Thus, when they join a group of their own volition, there may be a tension between what is asked of them by a tutor and their own ideas and plans. Where an adult is required to attend, s/he may actively resent being there at all, let alone be receptive to further direction by a tutor.

Alan Rogers[3] has recently suggested that the way(s) in which an adult perceives the power relationships with a tutor is the most significant difference between the teaching and learning of adults and children. The adult student will on occasion choose the 'adult as learner' role rather than that as 'equal adult with the tutor'. In these circumstances s/he will want the tutor to take on the role of 'adult as tutor' and to unambiguously organise and manage the learning and teaching. This will be particularly the case where the material is unfamiliar or difficult. At other times, the student will see him/herself as 'adult as adult' and will anticipate an equality with the tutor. Rogers argues for the approach 'that starts where they are', making use of formalised learning and of task-related learning according to group and individual needs.

KEY POINTS

- *The wisdom that adults possess – their knowledge and experience of the world – should be exploited to the benefit of all.*
- *Many adults can lack confidence in themselves as learners, especially in what they perceive to be formal educational settings.*

---

[3] Rogers, A. *What's the difference'* Adults Learning, Oct. 2003, 15, 2, 15–17

4 Some Expectations of Adult Learners

Adults have clear expectations about their tutors and of the courses they attend. Whilst their views may alter with experience, they need to be taken into account at all stages of the learning and teaching process.

1 Adults expect the tutor to know his/her subject. They do not expect encyclopedic knowledge and they will respect a tutor for saying that s/he doesn't know the answer to a particular question. However, they do expect tutors to demonstrate a firm grasp of the subject material, whether they are giving a talk, demonstrating a skill, facilitating a discussion, or providing individuals with the necessary feedback about their progress.

2 Adults expect the tutor to show enthusiasm for the subject, to exhibit a sense of eagerness to teach, and to care about students' learning achievements. They want to see the tutor model good practice, ably demonstrating the skills to be learnt or embodying the principles being espoused. Adult students expect tutors to 'practice what they preach'.

3 Adults expect the tutor to be a competent teacher and to employ the appropriate teaching skills when working with a group. They expect the tutor to have properly planned and prepared a session, to be a good communicator, to use a variety of teaching/ learning methods and resources, and above all, to manage the overall learning situation effectively to the benefit of all members of the group. Some adults may at first expect to be taught in old fashioned ways; they will remember being talked at in school and they may anticipate that similar approaches are still in use. People may initially be rather taken aback by requests to participate actively, to offer their experiences and knowledge, and to take responsibility for their own learning and achievements. (Roger's 'adult as adult' and 'adult as learner' dichotomy.)

4   Adults expect value for time spent – time spent for effort expended, for arrangements made and for fees paid. They anticipate decent surroundings and proper 'customer care'. They want to attend a course which is pitched at the right level, that is relevant to their needs and that accords with their existing capabilities.

5   Adults expect to work and to achieve something as a result. Whilst they may groan about the effort they are asked to make, they actually don't expect it all to be easy. Few adults attend for social reasons alone and it is unlikely they will stay away because realistic and attainable demands are made of them. They may, however, drop out where a course or tutor asks too little of them.

6   Adults expect to be told how well they are doing as individuals and as a group, whether they are studying a practical technique, a creative skill, a physical activity, a language, or an intellectual discipline. Feedback to students about their progress should include not only a yardstick of present success but also constructive and positive advice about what they can do to develop and improve the activity in which they are involved.

7   Adults expect to enjoy their learning. They are unlikely to give up time and money for long if the learning experience is dour and unexciting. Whilst it might not always be fun and 'joy unconfined', every learning experience should be positive, productive and an adult experience.

8   Adults expect their adult status to be recognised. Quite properly, they expect to be treated with respect and dignity on a course as elsewhere. They will not put up with harsh criticism, humiliation or being patronised; they do not want to be treated like children. They will vote with their feet if they do not find the equality of adulthood that is their right.

KEY POINTS

- *People expect to be treated with the equality of adulthood.*
- *People expect value for money which includes being taught by enthusiastic, competent and responsive tutors.*

5 Adult Motivation

Adults participate in lifelong learning for a variety of reasons. They can have more than one motive though they may have difficulty in articulating all of them.

1   Some common motives include those having to do with:

* vocational or professional development
    - to access some further learning opportunity
    - to obtain a qualification
    - to fulfil vocational requirements
    - to broaden vocational horizons and possibilities

* an aspiration of further learning or creativity
    - to develop a new/existing interest, idea or skill
    - to create something
    - to satisfy curiosity
    - to engage in the process of learning

* a personal development goal
    - to discover 'if I can/if I still can'
    - to enhance confidence in the subject
    - to enhance self-esteem
    - to gain the approval of others

* a social need
    - to meet like-minded others
    - to make social contact
    - to gain social self-confidence.

Whilst there are adults who initially attend to satisfy some pressing social need, perhaps someone has been recently widowed or has just moved into the area, practically everyone also has some educational purpose in mind. What are sometimes called 'soft' learning outcomes, such as growth in self confidence, are more often the goals of course providers rather than a stated objective of those who attend courses.

2   If people are to maintain an optimum level of learning motivation, they must identify and work towards realistic goals that are within their capabilities and then experience ongoing success. Constructive feedback – 'being told how you are doing and getting good ideas of what to do to make it better' – is a major component of this process.

3   There will be times when people's motivation is low and they feel discouraged. Membership of the group may not be as rewarding as first anticipated, parts of the course may seem especially difficult and they may be experiencing setbacks in their lives quite apart from anything the course might engender. As well as lack of purpose and failure to achieve, whether real or apparent, other disincentives to continue to learn include:

   –   a patronising and/or unfriendly tutor
   –   poor class organisation and management
   –   poor teaching
   –   little individual attention
   –   little recognition of adulthood
   –   an unfriendly atmosphere
   –   poor group support.

Many of these aspects are directly related to the attitudes and skills of the tutor and the atmosphere that s/he develops. Whilst an uncomfortable environment or inadequate resources are important issues, if the course is well run and managed by a skilful, enthusiastic and committed tutor, most adults are able to respond positively and maintain optimum levels of motivation to work and to achieve.

4   There are a numbers of barriers that can prevent someone from ever becoming an adult student. These are, firstly, situational barriers such as lack of time, lack of money and lack of child/

family care; secondly, dispositional ones including lack of self-confidence, feeling too old, lack of qualifications, previous educational failure; and finally, institutional barriers such as inconvenient location, inappropriate subjects, unsympathetic timetabling, high fees; a 'cold' atmosphere and unhelpful staff. Whilst most of these may be beyond your control as a tutor, you can influence the marketing of your courses and perhaps suggest modifications to the infrastructure that would make provision more accessible and user friendly. You certainly have a major role in developing and maintaining a positive, responsive and adult atmosphere within your own course.

5   People's preconceptions can determine their response to a course and to a tutor. They may have a view about what sort of course process is most appropriate for what they have in mind (where 'process' is the way in which a course is managed and run, and includes the tutor as an appropriate model of good practice). Thus goal-oriented individuals may initially react against group methods and activities that appear to lack direct relevance and/or purpose. They may feel they want more formal presentations by the tutor. Those individuals who are more concerned with personal development may be happier with a relaxed, informal approach and more active participation. Their choice would be for less didactic teaching and more 'sharing'.

6   Adults are motivated to learn, and learn best, when:

   –   they feel secure and they can try out things in safety
   –   their needs are being met in ways that they can see are relevant and appropriate
   –   they feel involved and engaged in their learning
   –   their active participation and contributions are encouraged and acknowledged
   –   they are provided with a variety of learning opportunities via a range of methods
   –   they know what they have to do, especially when they have been involved in the setting of realistic goals
   –   they know how well they are doing

    – they achieve some immediate as well as longer term success

    – they perceive that they are welcomed and respected as adults and as individuals.

7 A tutor's personal style, commitment and enthusiasm are major motivating factors in helping adult students continue learning. People respond to tutors who show genuine interest in and concern for their individual achievements, who support and encourage them as adult learners, and who interact with them on equal terms.

KEY POINTS

- *For some people, just returning to learning at all requires courage and is a significant achievement in itself.*
- *Whatever the initial motives may be, achieving some success 'now' will motivate further efforts to learn.*

6 The Pottery Class: an Adult Student's Experience

A number of studies have been carried out over the years looking at why adults drop out of classes. Whilst people do cease coming for personal and family reasons, not least the competing demands of work and busy lifestyles, others have different priorities and will let go of their class as a last resort. People also have a more discerning eye than some tutors may give them credit for. Follow up surveys of student drop outs have revealed a catalogue of poor teaching practices including tutors who are 'dull ... uninspiring ... anecdotal and self-centred ... don't notice or act upon class discontent ... lack organisation ... have little structure to their teaching and are hard to follow ... show no interest in their students or their learning'. The genuine account which follows was written by Sue, an adult student who enrolled in a class advertise as 'Pottery for All'. What she describes offers food for thought to all tutors of adults, regardless of subject or setting. You can compare your reactions to what she has to say with the suggestions we offer to Geoff, the pottery tutor. [7]

First Week.
When I arrived, the tutor was already there talking to the only other student present, a man. It was 6.45. They didn't speak to me. I wandered about the room reading notices. The tutor eventually did speak to me though all he said was that I wasn't dressed properly for pottery. I'd gone in my jeans and shirt so I immediately felt as if I'd got my satin evening dress on. As I surreptitiously took my rings off and put them in my bag I said I hadn't known what to expect on the first night and that I was in my old gear. People started coming in and the tutor greeted some of them; it was clear that he already knew them. When he began, he asked how many people had done pottery before and about half put up their hands. I felt a bit better; perhaps I wouldn't look such an absolute fool. There were 14 altogether, eleven women and three men.

The tutor introduced himself: 'I'm Geoff ... nothing formal', but he said that he couldn't attempt to learn our names. He started to demonstrate how to 'de-air' a lump of clay but he began before I realised what he was doing and I couldn't see properly. As he finished the demonstration he said that we didn't need to worry because the clay we would use had already been prepared! He warned us that he might use words that would be unfamiliar to us. I wanted to take notes, because I knew I wouldn't remember; but I didn't dare because nobody else did. He showed us how to make a hollow ball of clay and then turn it into a small pot. He suggested that those who had done it before might prefer to do something else – but he didn't say what and no one did. The whole demonstration lasted about 10 minutes and then we were asked to get on with it ourselves. Everyone tried to reproduce the kind of pot that he had made.

He went for coffee about 8.00 saying that students didn't usually take a break and preferred to work through. I made my first pot and then wondered what to do. So I made another – the same but smaller. And then another – same again but smaller still. He came back after about 20 minutes. He went to two students and advised them how they could improve their pots and then he wandered about the room a bit. He didn't come to look at my pots or those of the other people near me. Nobody in the class talked much though one young man on my table who had clearly done pottery before kept saying how relaxing it all was. I was getting more and more frustrated and would have liked to chuck some clay at the wall. The time dragged and I played about with more clay just to look as if I were doing something. I left at 9.00 feeling pretty flat wondering what I had achieved. I certainly hadn't established any kind of relationship with the tutor, though I had talked a bit to the people on either side of me. I saw others using wet sponges so I had copied them. I learned that if you don't get all the air out of the clay your pot will disintegrate in the kiln, and that the first firing is called biscuit firing. I could do what I had been told – which wasn't much – but I was aware of a lack of creativity. I drove home thinking how I could get my money back.

Second Week.

I expected that to-night's experience would be much the same as last week – but hoped it might be better. It wasn't! I arrived 10 minutes early to find the tutor on his own. He smiled and we chatted for a minute or two, so I began to feel a bit more relaxed than last week. More people arrived though we all sat in the same places as we had before. The tutor demonstrated another technique for making a pot – coiling. We were to make a round base and build up the sides with sausages of clay then smooth it out inside and out.

I felt like a contestant on a TV game show, particularly when mine kept *falling off the wheel. I laughed at my efforts but nobody else did. It was all very quiet and serious. So I shut up and got on with my pot. The shape seemed all right but again I found myself short of ideas about what to with it. I decided that I would ask the tutor for help when I needed it rather than wait for him to come round. He went off to coffee, so when he came back I asked him to have a look at my pot and give me some ideas about what to do as it was getting taller and taller. He gave me one suggestion which didn't seem to make sense so I ignored it! I carried on, though, but soon felt very depressed about my lack of creativity. Ten minutes before time, he told us how to wrap up our pots so that we could continue with them next week. Nobody seemed to have completed anything.*

I left feeling frustrated, though on the way home I found I was thinking more about what I could do with my pot next time than about the class itself. I decided that the only way was to look as some books on pottery and glean some ideas and information that way.

Third Week.
Fantastic! What a great night! I came out on a real high. I finished last week's pot and it hasn't turned out too bad at all. The girl sitting next to me asked a question about the type of clay we were using and the tutor immediately explained to us where the clay came from and described the various sorts there are as well as what kinds of articles are made from each. He then watched what we were doing with out pots and came round and showed us a different way. He came over later to see how I was doing. I finished the main shape and said I wanted to put on handles but didn't know how. He watched me as I tried to work it out and then said that I had the right idea and that he would do the first one for me. He worked with a great deal of skill. I watched fascinated as the handle just seemed to grow out of his fingers. I said he could do the second one as well but he said I should do it myself. I managed it and when he came back he picked up the pot and said 'Not bad at all. You've made a good job of it.' He spent time going round helping everyone and showing them how to do things – his enthusiasm was catching. When it was time to finish he told me what to do with my pot next time to finish it off.

I felt really enthused and excited. I had had a really constructive and profitable evening. The two girls at my table also said how much they had enjoyed the evening after the disappointments of the first two sessions. What a pity that this teacher was only a stand-in for the first teacher who had 'flu!

I went up to him at the end and said how much I had enjoyed the class. I said it was evident that he was enthusiastic about pottery. He replied that he loved his job and wanted everyone to get pleasure and satisfaction out of pottery. I told him that I appreciated the feedback we'd been offered – even where it was critical. He asked me if we didn't usually get it and I answered, 'No'. I said that on the other evenings I had gone home feeling very flat and though I was sorry to criticise, we were paying a lot of money for the course and we weren't getting what we needed. He asked if I could join one of his day-time classes and when I said I couldn't, he said 'Well, stick to it because you've done well tonight'. I came out feeling a million dollars. Even though I knew my pot was a bit cock-eyed, I'd made a start.

Fourth Week.

I feel flat again … last week's enthusiasm has gone. The original teacher is back and though I think he does try, he doesn't seem to have any spark about him. He kept on about how guilty he felt about missing a week. I felt guilty because I was sorry he had come back! He began by demonstrating how to make slabs of clay and how to make pots out of them, but he didn't generate any enthusiasm. After the demonstration he left the room for 15 minutes – though it wasn't coffee time – telling us to get on by ourselves. I noticed that quite a few people were helping each other, and that they did so whether he was there or not. When he did talk to individuals it seemed to me that he was chatting rather than talking about pottery. Before I got there I had decided that if the original teacher came back and the class wasn't any better I would pack it in and ask for my money back. But then I wouldn't get my pots back because they had still to be fired. So I didn't know what to do.

Fifth Week.

I'm not going anymore. I've got better things to do with my time.

Eight Week.

I'm still feeling pretty fed up about the whole thing. I haven't written to ask for my money back yet. I didn't know whether to invent an excuse for not going or whether to complain, so in the end I haven't done anything. I haven't been to collect my pots. I daren't.

I'm fed up because my expectations weren't met. They started pretty high and I had had a taste of how good pottery could be when we taught by the replacement teacher. It seemed that my initial motivation disappeared because of the personality and teaching style of the original tutor. He was much too casual, he didn't set any expectations and he didn't demonstrate commitment or enthusiasm. I think that adult students don't go to classes just for social reasons. They go to work and to achieve something. It takes a lot of energy and organisation to sort out the family and to be there regularly and on time. Once there, people want to get as much out of it as they can and the teacher is the key.

Did any more students drop out of the class or were they content just to use the facilities and be left alone to get on by themselves? Nobody wrote to ask me why I'd stopped going. What does the Centre do when a class folds, I wonder? Fees go up each year and it seems to me that the authorities should recognise their social and moral responsibilities and ensure that the service they offer is expert and value for money. If they are going to charge high fees, they should at least offer quality.

7 A Letter to Geoff ... and a *P.S.* to Dave

What follows is imaginary feedback, written to Geoff, Sue's pottery teacher. The points made here are the kinds of things that a quality assurance manager, a training course tutor, or an inspector from the Adult Learning Inspectorate – might well raise in a discussion with a tutor following an 'Observation of Teaching and Learning' [25] visit. The chances are that you don't teach pottery, but a number of the critical incidents described here will still apply to your subject ... and to your teaching ... and to you. So learn from a.n.other!

First Week.
When I arrived the tutor was already there talking to the only other student present, a man. It was 6.45.

Good that you are there early and sufficiently prepared and ready to talk to the early bird.

They didn't speak to me. I wandered about the room reading notices.

But what about Sue, the rather obviously new student? She would have welcomed a friendly 'Hello' from you. You could have found out her name, and in chatting to her, discovered her level of experience and what she was looking for.

No doubt the notices in the pottery studio put up by the day time teacher are of some interest. But a display put up by you – of pottery, books, photos, handouts, notices, etc, for your own adult students – would be more appropriate. Students can utilise any spare time they have to pick up ideas, learn 'how to', broaden their design horizons, extend their aspirations. You could even offer to lend your books against a signature. People rarely abuse the opportunity and they'll appreciate your interest in their learning and your open handedness.

The tutor eventually did speak to me though all he said was that I wasn't dressed properly for pottery. I'd gone in my jeans and shirt so I immediately felt as if I'd got my satin evening dress on. As I surreptitiously took my rings off and put them in my bag. I said I hadn't known what to expect on the first night and that I was in my old gear.

Whilst Sue might have been overdressed, this is what she thought would be appropriate. She says here that she was embarrassed that she'd got it wrong … and she must have felt stupid. A simple handout sent to intending students – or some notes attached to the course details in the brochure – can tell people what to wear, what to buy, what to bring, what books to look at, etc. They will welcome the contact with you, come better prepared, feel more comfortable and the class can get off to a flying start.

People started coming in and the tutor greeted some of them; it was clear that he already knew them.

Returning students would be pleased that you remembered them. It should also have been confirming for you to discover that they must have felt that what you did together on your previous course was of value to them and that they have come back. However, Sue (and other new students) felt an outsider and that she was joining an existing club. A 'Greetings to those who are here for the first time' would have been much appreciated.

When he began, he asked how many people had done pottery before and about half put up their hands. I felt a bit better; perhaps I wouldn't look such an absolute fool.

It *is* well worth your knowing the range of prior experience … and Sue felt reassured that she wasn't the only beginner. It is also important that you know what people hope to get out of the course. Being aware of their needs, expectations and aspirations, allows a tutor to tailor the course – and any given session – to best advantage. Clearly identifying their starting points also provides students with a base line from which they – and you – can plan their learning and subsequently judge their progress.

There were 14 altogether, 11 women and 3 men.

Class attendance is dependent upon a range of factors but check that your course is marketed in ways that are inclusive and encouraging of all. Is it welcoming to women *and* men, beginners *and* improvers, younger adults *and* the more mature, etc? Does it appear attractive to those who have never attended an adult course before, or may feel they lack creative and/or manual dexterity? Is anything implied that would discourage someone who has a disability, or who uses English as a second language from attending?

The tutor introduced himself: 'I'm Geoff … nothing formal' but he said that he couldn't attempt to learn our names.

A straightforward, personal introduction … but wouldn't the use of people's first names serve to confirm the informality you are after? As adults we want to be recognised as who we are and the use of our given names is a very obvious way of doing this. So you're bad at names; get some plastic badges and ask individuals what they'd like to be known as. Write them large enough for you to read from the front and ask people to wear them for your benefit. (Many will like being able to use each other's names, too!) Collect the badges in at the end of *every* session and lay them out when you arrive next time.

He started to demonstrate how to de-air a lump of clay but he began before I realised what he was doing and I couldn't see properly. As he finished the demonstration he said that we didn't need to worry because the clay we would use had already been prepared!

When you demonstrate, ensure that the group knows you're going to do so, and for what purpose, and that they can all see and hear. Sue doesn't mention it, but presumably you said under what circumstances 'de-airing' is important and why? (Your final comment does rather nullify the value of what you did, however.)

He warned us that he might use words which would be unfamiliar to us.

Every subject has its technical language, 'jargon' being those words that are unknown or not understood by the uninitiated. You are quite right to use proper terminology in context though you should always explain what each means.

I wanted to take notes because I knew I wouldn't remember but I didn't dare because nobody else did.

Some people learn best when they make some sort of written record and need to know from the start that they are welcome to do so. One helpful way is to prepare 'skeletal' handouts which give the main points but also have spaces for people to add their own notes or label diagrams. Do you prepare handout materials to support each session, to describe the techniques you're using, or a step by step instruction, and/or some historical aspect? When you do have them, say when you're proposing to distribute them.

He showed us how to make a hollow ball of clay and then turn it into a small pot. He suggested that those who had done it before might prefer to do something else – but he didn't say what and no one did. The whole demonstration lasted about 10 minutes and then we were asked to get on with it ourselves. Everyone attempted to produce the kind of pot that he had made.

Doubtless this procedure is an appropriate one to demonstrate, especially for the beginners ... and Sue was subsequently able to do it. However, since you must have known that your returnees had already practiced this skill, it would have been helpful to have suggested what they might have done instead. If, on the other hand, you had a good reason why the more experienced *should* make pots in this way, then why not share your rationale with them.

He went for coffee about 8.00 saying that students didn't usually take a break and preferred to work through.

Coffee breaks are problematic. As tutor, you may need a break and it is often beneficial for students to step back from their activities too. Yet they will have 'paid a substantial fee' and may not want to 'waste good time' nor 'stop on a winning streak'. So rather than your deciding what is to happen, negotiate with each group what they want. Those who want a coffee can go, and others not ... though you'll need to agree what *you* will do. Alternatively, a volunteer could collect ordered coffees and bring them back to the room ... or people could bring thermos flasks ... or you might provide a coffee box – kettle, coffee, milk and a kitty.

I made my first pot and then wondered what to do. So I made another, the same but smaller. And then another, the same again but smaller still. He came back after about 20 minutes.

Whilst you were gone, Sue (and others, presumably) had been beavering away on a production line. (By the way, 20 minutes = 1/6 of the total paid-for class time!) The fact that hers got smaller each time may indicate a lack of belief in what she was doing ... and why she was doing it. It may be that repetitive practice is beneficial, but students need to know that this is the case, and what to look for, and what to concentrate on, and what they are aiming for!

He went to two students and advised them how they could improve their pots and then he wandered about the room a bit. He didn't come to look at my pots or those of the other people near me.

Whilst it is difficult to get round everyone on every occasion they work on their own – and there were 14 of them in this group – people do expect feedback about what they are doing. Constructive feedback tells them that they are on the right lines, working to an appropriate standard and provides them with ideas of how to improve and develop. It is motivating and confirms that what is being attempted is worth while. People don't ask for equal time but they do expect fairness. Sue (and her neighbours) clearly felt neglected and probably stalled.

Nobody in the class talked much though one young man on my table who had clearly done pottery before kept saying how relaxing it all was.

Perhaps Sue didn't see that the quietness of the group might have been due to people's absorption in what they were doing. But it might also have been that some were feeling self-conscious, unsure of themselves as new members, and/or thought that talking 'wasn't quite the thing'. There is little reason why they shouldn't chat as long as it doesn't interfere with their work; it isn't school. Part of the role of tutor is to facilitate social interaction between group members. Not only does it make for a more relaxed and friendly atmosphere but it sets the stage for people to share problems, ideas, suggestions and skills. Learning from each other is of significant valuable; it is difficult to share with someone you don't know.

I was getting more and more frustrated and would have liked to chuck some clay at the wall. The time dragged and I played about with more clay just to look as if I were doing something.

Frustration, anger, boredom, low motivation and lack of purpose ... not the reactions to be hoped for, and certainly not those of a student who feels that s/he is achieving something worthwhile. Clearly, it has all gone wrong for Sue so far.

I left at 9.00 feeling pretty flat wondering what I had achieved. I certainly hadn't established any kind of relationship with the tutor though I had talked a bit to the people on either side of me. I saw others using wet sponges so I had copied them. I learned that if you don't get all the air out of the clay your pot will disintegrate in the kiln, and that the first firing is called biscuit firing. I could do what I had been told – which wasn't much – but I was aware of a lack of creativity.

Well, she says she had learnt something from you ... and vicariously from others, but she felt she hadn't achieved what she hoped for. Though she had made three pots, this was as a result of 'watch and then do', not quite her expectation of creativity. It would have helped if you had said something about the need to master the basic techniques and that one couldn't expect to be Claris Cliff on a first evening ... that what ever is made is a unique item however simple ... and what pleasure can be derived from the experience.

What kind of relationship might she – and others – have been seeking? Perhaps one based on your interest in her as an adult and as a learner, in her prior experience, in her reasons for coming, and in her progress. She might have shared with you her anxiety about attending the class ... and of being with more talented students ... and her poor manual skills. She did want to know about you ... and your enthusiasm for pottery.

I drove home thinking how I could get my money back.

Whether it is a hangover from schooldays and the image of 'the teacher' or a cultural reluctance to complain face to face, few students will say outright that they are dissatisfied and that the class (or the tutor him/herself) isn't what they had hoped for. They take the easier way out and vote with their feet even when a formal complaints procedure is available. Watch for the clues and cues that indicate what people are thinking about the class, as well as taking notice of their ongoing interest, motivation and achievement.

Second Week.

I expected that to-night's experience would be much the same as last week – but hoped it might be better. It wasn't! I arrived 10 minutes early to find the tutor on his own. He smiled and we chatted for a minute or two, so I began to feel a bit more relaxed than last week.

Whilst Sue wouldn't wait after the class last week, she came earlier this second time, and probably not by chance. Students often come early and stay on at the end in order to have a quiet word. She seemed to feel that she has benefited from making some direct contact with you ... and that she was willing to have another go.

More people arrived though we all sat in the same places as we had before.

People very quickly regard a place/seat/potter's wheel to be 'theirs'. We derive a sense of security from familiar places and situations, and this seems to apply to adult classroom positions as well! This isn't necessarily a problem unless: (a) you want to use small group methods and the same people end up with the same partners; (b) or an individual is a constant nuisance to near neighbours.

The tutor demonstrated another technique for making a pot – coiling. We were to make a round base and build up the sides with sausages of clay then smooth it out inside and out.

A 'watch me' demonstration followed by individual practice ... an appropriate way of working, though the methods you use and their order of use need to be varied week by week. There *is* an issue about the range of pottery skills and experience within the group, however. Hadn't last year's students done this already? Wouldn't it have been an idea to set them off on another/parallel activity of their own whilst you showed the technique to beginners? What is the particular benefit of the returnees watching you demonstrate the technique?

I felt like a contestant on a TV game show, particularly when mine kept falling off the wheel. I laughed at my efforts but nobody else did. It was all very quiet and serious. So I shut up and got on with my pot.

Sue was willing to have a go ... and to enjoy the making, the successes and any disasters, but she says she soon lost her zest. The group's mood would seem to have been overly serious, and whilst you can't order them to 'lighten up', it is part of your role to facilitate a friendly and adult atmosphere. This should be one that not only promotes learning, but also fosters a sense of shared enjoyment and achievement between collaborating adults. Fun *is* allowed in adult classes!

The shape seemed all right but again I found myself short of ideas about what to with it. I decided that I would ask the tutor for help when I needed it rather than wait for him to come round. He went off to coffee, so when he came back I asked him to have a look at my pot and give me some ideas about what to do as it was getting taller and taller. He gave me one suggestion which didn't seem to make sense so I ignored it! I carried on though I soon felt very depressed about my lack of creativity.

Sue began to use her own judgement about her work, but like all students, she wanted some feedback from you. Since you hadn't managed to get to her, she decided to be more proactive and ask for your guidance ... though she didn't apparently risk it until the second half of the session. Sadly, what you offered her doesn't seem to have met with her needs.

There is a helpful sequence that can be used for these 'one-to-one' dialogues. It typically begins with finding out what the student thinks about his/her work, then the identification of the main good/not-so-good aspects, leading to constructive help on one or two main features that the student can see are relevant and ones on which they can work.

Ten minutes before time he told us how to wrap up our pots so that we could continue with them next week.

Giving people a clear signal about 'time left', general actions to undertake, etc, is a good idea. 'Start on time and finish on time' is a good working maxim, though it means that a tutor must carefully manage the time and the learning opportunities in between.

Nobody seemed to have completed anything. I left feeling frustrated, though on the way home I found I was thinking more about what I could do with my pot next time than about the class itself. I decided that the only way was to look as some books on pottery and glean some ideas and information that way.

Had you anticipate that they would finish their pots, or did you plan on a two week project? If the latter, you should have warned the group. Sue was disconcerted that no one had finished, and personally frustrated at her own lack of more immediate success. She seemed determined to progress her work, however, and had identified how she might do so on her own. If you aren't able to devote time to all individuals in the class during every session, think about providing alternative strategies that would allow them to move on. You could offer 'what' and 'how to' handouts, for example, as well as loaning books and/or providing previously made *Blue Peter* examples. These could be looked at, learnt from, serve as models, be discussed between students as they share and learn from each other.

Third Week.
Fantastic! What a great night! I came out on a real high. I finished last week's pot and it hasn't turned out too bad at all.

You couldn't ask for more; a student who has achieved something to his/her own satisfaction and who has enjoyed – and learnt from – a session. Sue's excitement and motivation are palpable.

The girl sitting next to me asked a question about the type of clay we were using and the tutor immediately explained to us where the clay came from and described the various sorts there are as well as what kinds of articles are made from each.

A good idea to extend your answers beyond the requested facts and sketch in other relevant aspects. If it feels right, turn the question back to the student: 'What do you think might be the case? What use might it have? What else is it like? Could this be a way of ...?' Such incidental learning can be long lasting ... and vicarious learning – eavesdropping on what is said to others – can prove equally valuable.

He then watched what we were doing with our pots and came round and showed us a different way.

Keeping an observant eye on group progress as well monitoring individuals at work means that a tutor can suggest, guide, show, confirm and/or correct at a point when the whole group would benefit from a general piece of teaching, an announcement or an impromptu demonstration.

He came over later to see how I was doing. I finished the main shape and said I wanted to put on handles but didn't know how. He watched me as I tried to work it out and then said that I had the right idea and that he would do the first one for me. He worked with a great deal of skill. I watched fascinated as the handle just seemed to grow out of his fingers. I said he could do the second one as well but he said I should do it myself. I managed it and when he came back he picked up the pot and said 'Not bad at all. You've made a good job of it.' He spent time going round helping everyone and showing them how to do things – his enthusiasm was catching.

Sue makes it very plain that she valued the time you spent with her from a number of standpoints: you first watched to assess what she was doing ... then diagnosed and praised ... then demonstrated a technique ... and avoided being manoeuvred into doing it for her ... and came back to confirm her progress. As she says, you moved round the class to observe everyone and talk to them about their work. They will all have benefited, as she did, from the motivating effects of your enthusiasm for pottery as well as from their own achievements.

When it was time to finish he told me what to do with my pot next time to finish it off. I felt really enthused and excited. I had had a really constructive and profitable evening. The two girls at my table also said how much they had enjoyed the evening after the disappointments of the first two sessions. What a pity that this teacher – Dave – was only a stand-in for the first teacher who had 'flu!

Your individualised suggestion to her of how she could work on her pot appears to have rounded off a highly successful evening for her. (It is reckoned that humans – and animals for that matter – typically experience a strong drive to complete an unfinished task, at least where the desired goal is valued. So there!) Sue also makes it clear that she was not alone in her judgement of what a really worthwhile session you ran for them.

I went up to him at the end and said how much I had enjoyed the class. I said it was evident that he was enthusiastic about pottery. He replied that he loved his job and wanted everyone to get pleasure and satisfaction out of pottery. I told him that I appreciated the feedback we'd been offered – even where it was critical. He asked me if we didn't usually get it and I answered 'No'. I said that on the other evenings I had gone home feeling very flat and though I was sorry to criticise, we were paying a lot of money for the course and we weren't getting what we needed.

Dave, you may have guessed that the way you worked with these adults wasn't what they had been used to with Geoff. The fact that Sue came and spoke to you at the end reflects upon the relationship *you* built with the group. Your enthusiasm and your wish that other people should get equal delight from pottery were clearly evident ... and the group responded. Equally, your 'one to one' work was valued; it is of some significance that Sue says 'what we needed' rather than 'what we wanted'. People quite rightly expect value for money ... and for 'time spent' ... and for 'arrangements made to attend' ... and for 'effort put in'.

He asked if I could join one of his day-time classes ...

There's no reason why you shouldn't have suggested one of your classes. Indeed, students should be offered guidance and information about opportunities for progression.

... and when I said I couldn't, he said 'Well, stick to it because you've done well tonight'. I came out feeling a million dollars: even though I knew my pot was a bit cock-eyed I'd made a start.

There are plenty of ways of saying 'very good', and part of Sue's sense of achievement was a result of your positive comments about her cock-eyed pot. Whilst adults readily spot being patronised, we all value positive confirmation, especially from those who we rate as credible.

Fourth Week.
I feel flat again ... last week's enthusiasm has gone. The original teacher is back and though I think he does try, he doesn't seem to have any spark about him. He kept on about how guilty he felt about missing a week. I felt guilty because I was sorry he had come back!

Well, Geoff, she's saying how it was for her. Did you talk to Dave about how last week's class went and what he thought about your students? Did he give any indications that they seemed to want a bit more feedback about how they were doing … and individual help and guidance … and like all adult students, seem to value and respond to enthusiasm? Whilst it is unfortunate that you had to miss a class, it did provide you with an opportunity to talk with another potter about teaching and working with adults … and about a group of adults that you both know.

He began by demonstrating how to make slabs of clay and how to make pots out of them, but he didn't generate any enthusiasm.

There is a fair degree of acting in teaching, and one part of our craft is to show interest in what is being demonstrated, or discussed, or work on. It may not be to the personal taste of the tutor, but if we judge that it is something that our students need then we owe it to them to present it with *evident* enthusiasm and interest.

After the demonstration he left the room for 15 minutes – though it wasn't coffee time – telling us to get on by ourselves.

Your absence from the class is being adversely noticed. If there is good cause for your leaving, then share it with people. They will understand a valid reason … but actively resent a tutor's 'fag break' or other unjustified disappearances.

I noticed that quite a few people were helping each other, and that they did so whether he was there or not. When he did talk to individuals it seemed to me that he was chatting rather than talking about pottery.

Sue seems to have felt that there was something not quite right about people helping each other. In fact there is no reason why they shouldn't, and indeed, collaborative learning amongst adults is to be encouraged. However, you should watch out that home grown experts don't appear, since they can be offering advice that might be incorrect and/or at odds with yours. Take care that your students are not advising each other because *you* are not offering them what they need.

Before I got there I had decided that if the original teacher came back and the class wasn't any better I would pack it in and ask for my money back. But then I realised that if I did, I wouldn't get my pots back because they had still to be fired. So I didn't know what to do.

Fifth Week.
I'm not going anymore. I've got better things to do with my time.

At least one of your students is saying that the class wasn't providing her with what she wanted or expected, and that she was intending to 'vote with her feet'. There was an opportunity for you to reclaim her since she wanted her fired pots back, and this implies that what she had done was of significance to her. It is sad that she has decided to quit and you weren't able to change her mind. There are some lessons to be learnt here ... and they are writ clearly enough within her honest opinions.

Eighth Week.
I'm still feeling pretty fed up about the whole thing. I haven't written to ask for my money back yet. I didn't know whether to invent an excuse for not going or whether to complain, so in the end I haven't done anything. I haven't been to collect my pots. I daren't. I'm fed up because my expectations weren't met. They started pretty high ... and I had had a taste of how good pottery could be when we were taught by the replacement teacher. It seemed that my initial motivation disappeared because of the personality and teaching style of the original tutor. He was much too casual, he didn't set any expectations and he didn't demonstrate commitment or enthusiasm. I think that adult students don't go to classes just for social reasons. They go to work and to achieve something. It takes a lot of energy and organisation to sort out the family and to be there regularly and on time. Once there, people want to get as much out of it as they can and the teacher is the key. Did any more students drop out of the class or were they content just to use the facilities and be left alone to get on by themselves? Nobody wrote to ask me why I'd stopped going. What does the Centre do when a class folds, I wonder? It seems to me that the authorities should recognise their responsibilities and ensure that the service they offer is expert and value for money. If they are going to charge high fees they should at least offer quality.

To whom it may concern ...
Even a month later, Sue remains significantly dissatisfied, and the tragedy is compounded by her lack of confidence to do anything about it other than quit. Not only had she lost out on the much of the learning experience *and* the objects she created, but she may well not return to other lifelong learning provision as a result. She

makes her reasons plain and does so from the informed position of having been able to compare two different tutors. Whilst learning is what the student must do for him/herself, the provision and management of learning is the tutor's responsibility ... and in her eyes this has to do not only with teaching style and skills, but also with a tutor's commitment and enthusiasm. She, like other students, pays her fees and organise her life in order to attend; she is ready and willing to put considerable effort into her learning activities *if it seems worth it*. And this didn't.

Whilst Geoff must bear some of the blame for a poor course, his line managers must share in it too, for there are major quality assurance failures here. He could, and should, have been helped by supportive staff development. A regular class observation visit to review and advise on the teaching and learning is called for (O.T.L.), linked with continued professional development activities such as individual mentoring, targeted training events, subject tutor networking, and peer visiting with the likes of Dave. Geoff might not have the personal attributes that make for an inspiring tutor but proper professional help and guidance could help him develop a level of at least satisfactory competence.

And later ...

When Sue was asked later what she wanted from a tutor she said: '*Someone who can put the pennies in ... help me to discover what I can do ... and tell me how I'm doing*'. When asked why she didn't say anything to Geoff, her pottery tutor, she replied: '*Well, I would never! (sic) It's up to him to know how to teach ... not for me to tell him. He should know!*'

... and this book tries to addresses much of what Geoff should have known ... and should have done.

ADULT TEACHING

When people are asked what makes for a good course for adults they usually identify similar factors. Their views can be categorised into three major groups.

The first has to do with course design. People describe a good course as one being relevant to their needs with clear statements of purpose and appropriate content presented at the right level and pace. In addition, they value a variety of interesting teaching and learning methods, together with opportunities to try out what they have learnt with feedback about how they are doing.

The second category might be called 'principles, values and tutor style'. What is of importance to people here is that they are treated in adult ways, their experience is welcomed and valued, they actively participate, and that they feel at ease with each other and with what is taking place within the group. They believe that tutors should be enthusiastic and enjoy what they do, sensitive to the needs of individuals, professionally competent as teachers and subject specialists, and willing to share as equals in the life of the group.

Finally, people itemise a range of factors which have to do with efficient organisation and administration, such as marketing and pre-course information, the quality of the materials, time-keeping and attention to detail, as well as domestic issues such as physical access, a clean and comfortable environment and the availability of decent refreshments.

In summary, adults say that a good course or session is one that helps them engage in relevant learning experiences in a variety of interesting ways with the help of a responsive and supportive tutor. Above all, they expect a good course – and tutor – to acknowledge their adulthood. The rest of this book is about how we as tutors can respond to these quite reasonable expectations of the people we work with.

II Planning for Learning

Introduction

It must be evident to every teacher of adults that actual face-to-face work is only part of the business of teaching. Planning and preparation are as much prerequisites for a teaching/learning event as are assessment and evaluation during and after it. There are no short cuts in this process. As a tutor you will need to determine what it is that people need, want and for what purposes. From such analyses, in which the opinions of adult students themselves play a critical part, you will be able to identify what you need to teach, what methods to employ and what equipment and resources to use. Further analysis of what took place will help identify what students actually achieved, what should be done on the next occasion the group meets, and the ways in which the session could be improved another time.

The elements of preparation and planning can be represented in a simple diagram, Illustration 3. The following pages deal with each in turn, though the first two chapters consider the underpinning processes of equal opportunities and of consultation and negotiation.

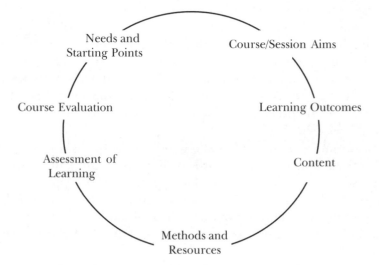

Illustration 3: Preparation and planning for teaching

8 Equal Opportunities

Equal opportunities have to do with ensuring everyone's right to appropriate and accessible education and training. Many people – women, the elderly, the less affluent, members of ethnic-minority communities, people with disabilities, people with learning difficulties – have been educationally disadvantaged and have missed out on many learning opportunities. The adult and community learning sector continues to make efforts to remove remaining barriers to learning, but with the law becoming more precise about non-discriminatory practices, tutors are being seen to have an increased role in this process of making access possible for all.

1   Find out what is being done at organisational and management levels to provide equal access and opportunities. Read your institution's equal opportunities policy and statements of student entitlement. Check how courses – especially your own – are being marketed and publicised. Do course times take account of school hours, public transport and holidays including religious and cultural ones? What about access arrangements for the elderly and people with disabilities, the provision of crèche and playgroup facilities, the provision of information and guidance, the flexibility of enrolment procedures, the fee arrangements for the unwaged and those on low incomes? If you, or your group, identify any shortcomings, make appropriate representation to the management.

2   The law on disability discrimination has been strengthened and this places responsibility upon course providers and the owners of the venues where courses are held, including field trip sites. The definition of disability includes physical disability, mental impairments including learning difficulties and clinically well-recognised mental illness, sensory impairment, and progressive/ cumulative conditions. Institutions – and this includes tutors – are expected to make adjustments for a student's disability including:

- administrative and assessment procedures, with extra time for the completion of assignments
- course content and the potential to substitute part of a course
- physical features of all premises, from ramps to hearing loops
- teaching arrangements such as visual displays, ease of lip reading, optimal seating positions for those with sensory impairment and additional help for dyslexic students
- alternative formats such as large print, Braille, and audio tapes
- communication and support services such as interpreters, readers, signers and carers.

3   Think about how you offer your course. If you normally teach a sequence of weekly sessions, consider what other formats might be possible which would increase access to potential students. What about a taster session, a weekend school, a roll-on-roll-off course, evenings instead of day and *vice versa*, a course in an outreach centre, community centre or local hall rather than in college or school premises, or perhaps a group for women only. If you were to change the emphasis and/or style of your course's publicity material it might attract a wider range of potential students; a change of title might also attract a greater diversity of people.

4   The ways in which you physically organise your teaching group as well as how you plan and prepare your course should take account of the physical and learning support needs individual students may have. For example, those who have a hearing or visual impairment should be offered optimum positions, whilst individuals who attend with personal helpers should be accommodated in ways which they feel best suit their particular needs. You must also ensure that the methods, course materials, resources and equipment are potentially useable by everyone. Carry out a risk assessment to ensure that your classroom equipment and resources are safe and 'fit for use' by everyone. Identify how you – and the group – can aid your student colleagues who initially may be less able to participate fully, and thus help them to achieve their learning aspirations.

     There are also extra-classroom features of importance to all students. These include the availability of refreshment, cloakrooms, sitting areas, library, IT facilities, and the resources centre. Is everyone aware of them and able to get to them easily? Do people feel at ease using them, and have you given them space on your course to do so? Try to see that students' personal as well as educational needs are being catered for.

5 Consider your own attitudes towards and knowledge about the variety of people you teach. The ways you speak and behave will say something about you, your perceptions and expectations of your students. You may be aware – and so may they – that your reactions vary towards students of different ages and of different abilities, to men and to women, to those from different ethnic and/or cultural backgrounds, or to those of a different sexual orientation. As a tutor, you have a professional duty to behave in non-biased ways that are acceptable to all. This means recognising that every adult is of equal worth irrespective of ethnicity, gender, ability, background or disposition, and working with each person to the best of your ability in order to further his/her achievements.

6 There is no magic formula. You must undertake a continuous process of analysis and reflection on what you do and how you do it to ensure that you are giving everyone a chance to surmount any personal barriers they may be facing and to engage with your subject.

  – Take care that the language and references that you and your students use are not offensive. Avoid terms that have negative over/undertones of race, ethnic origin, gender, sexual orientation, culture, age or disability. Use non-offensive words and phrases yourself, and suggest alternatives to members of the group should they use inappropriate language.

  – The examples and images that you use, whether in speech, visual displays or in written materials, should reflect and value the diversity of people. Try to ensure that the examples and experiences that you elicit and value from your students also reflect this variety. If they are restrictive or mono-cultural, offer additions of your own to extend people's awareness of the realities around them.

    – Sensitively challenge members of the group where they inadvertently say or do things that are inappropriate/unacceptable. At the same time, insist on zero tolerance of bullying, personal harassment, racist and other discriminatory references, as well as inappropriate social behaviour.

7   Providing everyone with individually appropriate access to your subject matter and helping them to achieve personal success is not easy. There is much current talk about the importance of differentiation – the matching of learning and teaching approaches to help all students reach their full potential regardless of their starting points. As the chapter on needs and starting points [10] indicates, knowing what these are can help you design individualised learning opportunities and constructive feedback whilst maintaining a sense of integration and group identity. You may need to help individuals recognise and surmount the additional educational barriers they experience or perceive 'because I am a woman ... black ... hard of hearing ... left school at 15 ... suffering from the effects of a stroke'.

8   Remember, however, that you are not working alone. Your institution will have tutor support procedures in place so make use of them. Nevertheless, the expectations that you personally have of your adult students, their potential and achievements, should relate to them as individuals. Act in accordance with the belief that change and development are possible, and that your role as tutor is to do all that you can to assist this process for everyone you work with.

KEY POINTS

- *Demonstrate a commitment to equal opportunities for all through everything that you say and do in your work with adults.*
- *There is only one key point ... and you've just read it!*

9 Consultation and Negotiation

Involving students in course decision-making recognises their equality as adults, as well as increasing their interest, commitment, motivation and learning. Discussion between group members and a tutor about course aims and learning outcomes, the way a course is planned and organised, subject content, the learning/teaching methods to be used, the manner in which achievement is to be assessed and the course evaluated, demonstrates a commitment to student responsibility for, and ownership of their own learning.

1 Three processes can be involved, either separately or together. In the first – informing – the tutor states that something is or has to be so and gives appropriate reasons. In the second – consultation – the tutor checks things out with the group but retains the option of whether or not to modify his/her initial proposals. In the third – negotiation – the decision to adopt a particular direction or to make a change is a mutual one, agreed by the group and tutor together. The different opinions that tutors hold about the use of consultation and negotiation with adult groups may reflect their implicit beliefs about the nature of the tutor/student power relationship as well as the contractual implications of a published course description. Their attitudes may also be influenced by their judgments of the likely level of a group's existing subject knowledge and people's prior educational experience.

2 All consultation and negotiation take place within the parameters of institutional regulations, health and safety demands, risk assessment, timing and environmental constraints, the availability of resources, syllabus and/or examination requirements, the inherent demands of the subject discipline and a tutor's own capabilities. Certain aspects of a course or session may simply not be 'up for grabs' and in such instances you can only inform, relaying the relevant details with appropriate explanation. However, it ought to be possible to strike a balance between those

aspects of the course which are 'for information only', those on which you can consult, and those which are fully negotiable.

3   The critical point about *consultation* is that the final decision is yours. You may want to know what the group thinks about taking a particular approach to the subject, the inclusion of a specific topic, or a way of working. 'This is what I propose we should do … and my experience suggests … for these reasons … because of these circumstances. What do you think … for knowing your feelings will help me decide exactly what we should do?' The implicit message is that you will take note of their opinions and feelings but remain the final arbiter.

4   *Negotiation* – where power is shared – cannot be undertaken from a position of relative ignorance. People must know something about the topic under consideration and the issues involved if they are to share in the responsibility of decision making. They must also be aware of the consequences of a particular decision: 'if *A* is chosen, then *B* has to be forfeited'. The process of negotiation, and to some extent consultation, is likely to prove strange to many adult students and upsetting to some. It will not have been a feature of their previous educational experiences and some will still see the tutor as 'authority'. Where this is the case, introduce negotiation with care: too much, too soon can be counter-productive.

5   If your group is to offer their consultative views and/or be empowered to undertake negotiation of some or all of the curriculum, its organisation and management, you will need to initiate safe, non-risky procedures to enable this to happen.

   –   Where your group is unfamiliar with the concept of negotiation, or does not possess the knowledge to make a decision, *consult* them about content and ways of working but begin to *negotiate* some of the more practical issues. You could, for example, agree start times; behavioural ground rules, coffee breaks, and/or homework. As the course progresses, propose they negotiate some other aspects 'now we've tried some of them out'.

– Undertake a sequence of activities which will help group participants recognise their existing knowledge as well as lead them to identify their learning needs. Such a procedure carried out during the first couple of sessions may provide them with sufficient knowledge to engage in negotiation and to take informed decisions with you about what is to be subsequently done during the course.

– Where you judge people possess the appropriate knowledge on which to base their judgments, you could contact them before the course begins and ask them to propose/choose the topics and procedures they would like to see included (see [12] below). You can then produce an overall structure based on strength of demand, and present it to them for discussion/confirmation when you meet together at the first session.

– Where a group is able to engage in full negotiation from the outset – and wants to do so, face to face – you will need to devote the first part of the course to the process. Whilst it can take an inordinate amount of time and lead to periods of intense frustration, the effects in terms of shared responsibility and commitment to both individual and group learning can be considerable.

6 All the following are potentially negotiable, some rather more easily than others:

– course/session aims and learning outcomes
– subject content
– order and structure of the subject content
– ways of teaching and learning
– student participation
– student work/assignments
– assessment and evaluation
– attendance requirements
– the environment (venue, classroom layout)
– times and timing (start/finish, coffee breaks, etc)

- AVAs and resources
- student materials supply
- social activities.

Whatever the subject being negotiated, monitor the discussion and keep the emotional temperature down. You should provide any information needed, point out the potential results of a particular proposal and indicate aspects/topics that may have been ignored or inappropriately discarded. Keep the group in touch with the subject's rationale and accepted procedures as well as making your own contribution about what you believe might or might not/should or should not be included. The group will want to know your preferences and hear what you think about their proposals, and, since the decision is a shared one, you do need to offer your 'ha'porth'. (It is a moot point whether your tutorial vote should be of equal weight to that of the group or just one of many. Perhaps you should negotiate this too!)

7   Negotiation carries shared responsibility for its results. Be sure the group recognises that present decisions may not benefit them in the ways they intended or foresaw, and that some later renegotiation may be called for. At the end of the discussion, you should summarise what has been agreed, make sure that everyone understands the implications involved, and then set about implementing the group's decisions.

It may be that neither you nor the group has the power to enact a desired modification. In such circumstances, you can carry on the process of negotiation on behalf of the group with those who have such power, ie institutional managers or those with responsibility for the subject and its standards.

8   If all this talk about negotiation frightens you, reflect for a moment. The chances are that you are already doing it though you and your students may know it as 'setting ground rules', 'agreeing what we'll do next time', 'discussing our next move' or something similar. So it might not be so novel after all.

KEY POINTS

- *Share responsibility for the course with students; they will be more committed to making it work as a result.*
- *Involve students in making decisions right from the start.*

10 Needs and Starting Points

Planning for learning begins at the point of needs analysis: what is it that intending learners need at their particular levels of development within a subject area to achieve the desired learning outcomes? Such information helps determine the concepts, knowledge, procedures and skills with which they should engage. If a subject has a representative body or is part of a national curriculum, then a series of syllabuses, course guidelines and assessment procedures should be available. Whilst these materials are of significant value to the tutor, they cannot take into account all the particular needs, expectations and aspirations of a group or of each individual. Thus, even where tutors have the benefit of such curriculum details, they will still need to find out about the particular needs and starting points of students and to use this knowledge to inform both overall course planning and the differentiated teaching and learning that may be called for.

1   There are a number of ways by which you might identify the needs of the particular group of adults you are to work with. You could:

   –   attend the enrolment session and talk with potential students. Ask them what they hope to gain from the course and what expectations they have of themselves, of the course and of you, the tutor
   –   write to enrolled students before the course commences and ask them about their expectations and hopes. You could include a draft course outline and ask them to comment on it, or come to the first session prepared to make suggestions for additions and alternatives
   –   hold an informal pre-course meeting and seek to identify what people want
   –   run a taster session or a one-day school and build a section into it where you ask participants to give their opinions, preferences and expectations for the course which is to follow
   –   make contact with previous students and ask for their

judgments. 'On reflection, what would you have found more useful ... helpful! ... was worthwhile ... enjoyable?'
-   talk with other experienced teachers of your subject and find out what they do with groups working at a similar level.

2   It may well be that it is impracticable for you to make prior contact with intending members of a new group, not least because you won't know who is going to turn up. So instead, you could initiate an informal, non-threatening discussion during the first session to ascertain what people already know and can do, what they hope to achieve and how they hope to achieve it. Bear the following in mind:

-   It is a good working principle to start on some interesting and worthwhile content as soon as possible in a first session. Whilst adults recognise the need for dealing with administrative and organisational matters, not least the fire escapes and other health and safety issues, they have come to engage with the subject. So paradoxically, our suggestion is that you do some content with them even before any of the needs analysis we are discussing here! Select a short topic such as some recent findings, a new technique, or a newspaper article, which will engage those who may already know something as well as those who don't. Work in interactive ways that will encourage everyone, including beginners, to give an opinion, draw deductions, suggest an alternative example, etc. What people say and do, the answers they give and the questions they ask, will give you valuable clues about what is 'quite new to me ... quite familiar ... that's what I'm interested in ... that's what I want to learn about'.

-   Asking individuals to declare their experience of the subject and their learning needs and expectations in front of an unknown group can be intimidating. This will be particularly the case if those who have spoken before are perceived as being 'so knowledgeable' and 'so confident'. Minimise individual risk by asking people to work informally with a couple of partners. Suggest that once they have introduced themselves they discuss such things as why they've joined the course, what their particular subject interests are, what they hope to achieve, and any worries or concerns they have. (Monitor these conversations, by the way!)

– A minimal way of gaining an impression of what has been discussed is to ask for a show of hands in response to a tariff of questions: 'How many people have studied the subject before ... have read any books on it ... know something about the basic techniques ... would find it useful to start at the beginning?' Whilst most people will feel happier about declaring their experience having once discussed it with a couple of others, it may still remain a problem for some. So ask each group to share the sort of things *they* were discussing and what *their* consensus is.

– In addition to sensing the general feeling, plan to get round everyone at some stage during the first or second session and talk to them individually. You could do this whilst they work on a subject-related task or activity, and/or whilst they are completing enrolment forms and other required paperwork.

3 The course provider may have instituted a more formalised procedure for recording individual starting points and progress. Such student profiles typically seek information about:

– physical needs: eg room access and seat positioning, large print handouts and/or audio taped notes, specialist equipment
– learning support needs: eg a support worker, an interpreter/ translator/signer
– help with reading, writing, maths, or exams
– financial support needs
– subject starting points: eg totally new, prior knowledge and skills, activities undertaken, courses attended, qualifications held
– preferred ways of learning: eg learning and teaching methods, visual or written material
– the goals to which they wish to work (their personal learning outcomes)

- 'anything else you'd like to tell us so that we can help you learn better'.

4 Requests for details about starting points may well be embedded in a larger 'Staged Process' of recognising and recording progress and achievement. This methodology has been developed as a way of tracking 'distance travelled' by students on non accredited courses, a viable alternative to the formal assessment evidence which accredited courses provide. The elements of the stage process include:

- clearly stated programme aims
- initial assessment of student starting points
- identification of challenging learning outcomes
- recognition and recording of progress and achievement
- end of programme leaner self-evaluation, tutor summative assessment, and review of overall progress and achievement.

5 The description of people's starting points, learning needs and personal aspirations will clearly be of use to you in your course planning and preparation, and in your subsequent work with each individual and with the group. You can check the course aims and planned learning outcomes with the group and match these with each individual's hoped-for learning outcomes and aspirations. You can help individuals set realistic personal goals and clarify any additional learning support that they require. You will be able to work with them differentially – a newly-coined term for doing what good tutors have always tried to do – namely helping individuals reach their full potential from where ever they are starting.

You certainly should be planning to provide individualised work for those who have particular needs, whether these are extension activities for those who need to be stretched, or alternative materials at a different level of difficulty for those who find it less easy. You may well have to spend more time with some individuals than others, though you need to be fair with your time overall.

6 If adequate provision for pre-course information and guidance has been made, then the disparities between individuals within a group *may* not be great. Though this does not mean that differentiation, the use of sub-groups and individualised attention are no longer necessary, integrated plenary group teaching will continue to have a place on your course. But bear in mind the following:

- watch for, and act upon, the cues and clues of students experiencing difficulties as well as finding it too easy
- give time and attention to individuals at their requests
- reduce individual exposure and risk
- help individuals recognise and value their successes
- invite individuals to contribute their experience and skills at times and in ways that match their capabilities
- explain things in more than one way; show and tell, explain and do
- use examples that relate to people's experience
- use a range of methods, resources and materials
- involve people with questions, simple tasks, group work and practical activities
- encourage group interaction to promote learning from others, the development of self-confidence and growth in social relations
- encourage partnerships and working together.

KEY POINTS

- *Find out what your intending students already know and can do, as well as what they hope to gain from the course.*
- *Be conscious of the learning needs of each of your students as they alternate from being an individual learner, to small group partner, to member of the full group.*

---

11 Aims and Learning Outcomes

Much has been written about aims, objectives and outcomes in teaching and learning though most of it will not concern us here. This is fortunate as there is a raft of concepts and terms involved – teaching and learning aims and purposes; teaching, learning, expressive and behavioural objectives; teaching and learning goals; real, intended, desired, and delayed learning outcomes, and so on – and the distinctions between them soon becomes pretty esoteric. Nevertheless, in planning a learning event, thought must be given to two levels of description – purposes (aims), and what people are to achieve (learning outcomes). Unless tutor and students are clear about what they are trying to do, they can't know how to set about doing it, let alone be in a position to decide whether they have attained anything worthwhile at the end.

1   Aims represent a learning event's aspirations; they are statements of intent, indicating the overall purpose of a course or programme (and indeed a session). They are usually long-term, expressed in general terms and do not lend themselves to easy evaluation. The purposes they address include one or more of:

   – to impart information, knowledge or ideas
   – to improve understanding
   – to develop interest
   – to increase the ability to think or develop self-expression
   – to modify attitudes, beliefs or sense of value
   – to encourage behavioural change
   – to enhance skills or physical co-ordination
   – to stimulate action.

2   The language of aims includes such words as inform, broaden, appreciate, understand, develop, and they are typically written from the viewpoint of what the event – or tutor – will try to do. 'The purpose of this course is to help participants to know ... to achieve ... to respond to ... to develop ...' something or other.

The aims for a road safety course for adult cyclists might be: 'to increase the personal safety and cycling skills of course participants, and to promote their awareness of, and their reactions to, the behaviour of other road users'. The aims of a training day for lay magistrates might be: 'to enhance sentencing decision-making by developing magistrates' knowledge and use of their sentencing powers'. However, this language is a bit stilted – fine for a submission to a line manager but rather remote to students. There is a lot to be said for a more informal style, especially where the aims are to be primarily read by students. 'This art history course aims to help you identify and distinguish between the work of individual painters and between different types of paintings of the period' … and … 'the purposes of this psychology course are to give you an understanding of why people think and act as they do in social situations, and to help you to develop some insights into your own attitudes, reactions and behaviour'. Note, however, that aims do not say what participants will actually be able to do but what the course will try to provide.

3   In addition to the *course* aim(s), an equivalent statement is needed to set out the overall purpose of an individual *session*. Many tutors employ the same sort of language for session aims as they do for course aims. Using the cycling example again, a session aim might be: 'to improve the/your recognition of the more dangerous cycling manoeuvres and to develop appropriate safety strategies'. A session aim on a psychology course might be: 'to introduce (you to) the concept of pro-social behaviour and to examine the reasons why bystanders do and do not go to the aid of victims'. (Some institutions ask that the purpose of a session be expressed in terms of planned student behaviour eg 'participants will recognise the more dangerous cycling manoeuvres and develop appropriate safety strategies'. Strictly speaking, such statements are descriptions of on-course activity rather than aims.)

However you choose to do it, take the time to create a clearly expressed statement(s) of what the course – and each session – is about which means something to you and to your students, not only for their guidance but also because it will direct your planning. Use the lead phrase: 'the purpose of this session is to …'

4   Learning outcomes (LOs), on the other hand, are descriptive statements about planned learning achievement, the hoped-for changes in the student. They describe the benefits that should accrue from students' new-found knowledge, understanding, work and practice which happen during a session (and a course). They are the level of description which says what the student will be actually be able to do, think, feel or say as a result of the planned learning/teaching event. They should be expressed using action verbs including those in Illustration 4.

5   Learning outcomes have the practical functions of helping to structure a learning/teaching event, determining the detailed planning and providing a basis for subsequent assessment procedures. It is said that learning outcomes should be based upon the mnemonic S.M.A.R.T., i.e. specific – measurable – achievable – realistic – time-bounded. Certainly, learning outcomes should not only describe the desired behaviour but ideally the conditions under which their attainment is to be demonstrated, and the criteria for such success. Consequently words such as know, really know, have a working knowledge of, have a good grasp of, understand, really understand, appreciate, appreciate the significance of, be aware of, and be familiar with, etc, are all quite inappropriate and should *never* be used in learning outcome statements.

6   When you write learning outcomes, use the lead phrase 'the student (or you) will be able to ...' In the example of a cycling safety session, one learning outcome might just be: 'you will be able to mount your bicycle from the kerbside and check for oncoming traffic without falling off!' Another might be: 'you will be able to give the correct hand signals for left turn, right turn and straight on to an observer positioned in front'. A third might be: 'you will be able to explain the safety requirements for front and rear lights and for reflectors as specified in the Highway Code'. On a lay magistrates' training event: 'participants will be able to recognise and describe the likely effects of a given sentence on an offender, making reference to re-offending rates'. As a student on a social psychology course: 'you will able to draw

Knowledge		Comprehension		Application	
define	outline	classify	interpret	apply	illustrate
describe	present	cite	judge	assess	include
enumerate	quote	compare	justify	chart	inform
identify	recall	convert	locate	choose	modify
label	recognise	defend	name	collect	participate
list	reproduce	describe	order	compute	perform
match	select	discuss	outline	construe	predict
measure	sequence	estimate	paraphrase	construct	prepare
name	state	exemplify	predict	demonstrate	provide
organise	write	explain	report	determine	relate
		formulate	represent	develop	report
		generalise	restate	discover	select
		give	review	explain	show
		example	summarise	establish	transfer
		identify	trace	extend	use
		illustrate		extrapolate	verify

Analysis		Synthesis		Evaluation	
analyse	examine	adapt	modify	appraise	evaluate
break down	identify	alter	model	argue	identify
categorise	illustrate	argue	negotiate	assess	interpret
characterise	infer	categorise	plan	attack	judge
classify	justify	combine	précis	choose	justify
compare	limit	compile	present	compare	predict
conclude	point out	compose	progress	contrast	prove
contrast	prioritise	construct	propose	conclude	rank
correlate	research	create	rearrange	criticise	reorganise
criticise	restate	derive	reconstruct	critique	reframe
diagnose	relate	design	relate	decide	select
differentiate	resolve	develop	revise	defend	support
discriminate	select	discuss	select	determine	value
distinguish	separate	explain	suggest	discriminate	weigh up
elucidate	summarise	formulate	summarise		
		integrate	synthesise		

Illustration 4: Words to use when writing learning outcomes

inferences and conclusions from psychological data, evaluating your findings against those reported in relevant literature'.

Think out exactly what your students are to achieve by the end of a session and write these planned-for learning outcomes in ways that allow you and the student to make some judgment as to whether or not they have been achieved. Once you are clear what they are, plan the session – selecting the content, choosing the best methods, identifying the resources, working out how to monitor achievement – so that your students will be able to do what is intended. Remember that your function as a tutor is to plan (and teach) the learning opportunities which will best enable people to achieve the agreed learning outcomes. Time spent thinking out learning outcomes – and talking them through with your group – really will pay handsome dividends in terms of their learning and achievement, your planning and teaching, and your mutual feelings of success.

7   Not every learning outcome resulting from a particular session may have been planned – and some that are planned may not be observable until later. In the cycling safety example, it may be that as a result of a course or particular session, some car-driving students may become more aware of the sense of danger and physical exposure experienced by bicycle riders. As a consequence, they may behave in much more courteous ways to the cyclists they encounter on the road. Students on an art history course might find themselves looking and reacting to works of art from other periods in new ways, perhaps looking at less preferred genres more positively. Such unanticipated results are known as 'windfall' outcomes.

8   You may remain quite unaware of some of the more personal, 'expressive' outcomes that individual students achieve, though these can be highly significant to them. A newly-acquired sense of confidence may help a cyclist enjoy greater personal and meaningful contact with nature and the countryside. As a consequence of studying people's motivation and behaviour, a psychology student might find him/herself being rather more empathetic to family members, especially those previously cared

for rather less! Hope that all your students achieve some personally valued, expressive learning outcomes beyond those you – and they – may initially have planned.

KEY POINTS

- *Specify aims in language that will tell people whether or not the course is for them.*
- *Write smarter learning outcomes by using the phrase 'By the end of the session students (you) will be able to ...' and so avoiding words such as 'know', 'understand', 'appreciate'.*

---

12 Subject Content

Deciding what the subject content should be for a particular course or session and then putting it into a teaching/learning sequence would seem relatively uncomplicated. Tutors are well-versed in their subject and whilst they may not be experts in everything they will know where to go for the necessary information. Similarly, most have acquired the critical skills within their particular area and though their own performance might not be perfect every time, they know how the activity should be carried out. Yet knowing one's subject does not of itself make either the selection or the structuring of course content that straightforward. Whilst it would be unrealistic to provide specific guidelines for the scores of different subjects taught to adults, some general principles apply.

1   Tutors are often prisoners of their subject traditions and their own training within them; they take what they learnt and how they learnt it to be the model of what *they* should do. Yet rethinking your subject from an adult learner's view point may be a rather better starting point. Ask yourself what are the really important tenets and skills that students *need* to know and/or do at their particular starting points? It would *nice* if they followed all the major avenues and interesting byways of your discipline, but you should be aiming to provide them with those important principles, knowledge and skills, set out in an appropriate order, that they *need* at their particular stage of development.

2   As the chapter on aims and learning outcomes demonstrates, you should be quite clear about the purpose and scope of the course before you start selecting detailed content. What is it trying to do ... what is the purpose or aim of the course or a particular session? Are you proposing an introductory overview or a detailed analysis of a particular area ... do you wish to change overall behaviour or modify particular opinions ... to deepen conceptual understanding ... or to develop transferable practical skills? Simplistic though it may seem, once you decide upon the

course aims and, critically, equate them with the likely needs, interests and aspirations of intending students, the content begins to emerge. It becomes clearer still once you have taken the next step and determined the learning outcomes – what will people actually be able to do (or think or feel or say) by the end – since this begs the question of what knowledge, understanding and skills, they need *if* they are to achieve the learning outcomes. Thus: 'if they are to be able to do Z, they will need to know about X and have some practice of Y ... so I'll need to tell them/ provide a handout/let them work in groups on/ask them to research x^1, x^2 and x^3, then let them practice/write a draft/work together on y^1 and y^2. They will then be in a position to experiment/discuss Z and then do it for real. Bingo!'

Be aware that this does not suggest that you have to teach everything from first principles. People don't need to understand everything about a topic to deal with a current issue. They are adults with knowledge, experience and expertise in other content areas and may well be able to transfer concepts and ideas from other related areas, as well as taking some things on trust. It is our contention that it is often much better to draw necessary theory from practice and experience rather than the other way round.

3   If you carry out such an 'if this, then what ... if that, then how' approach to content selection, taking account of how it will seem from the adult student's standpoint, you should end up with an outline course structure and sequence, a clear indication of the necessary content, and some pointers to methods. Nevertheless, err on the side of less content rather than more. Whilst it *is* quite a good idea to have prepared more material than you think you might need, resist the temptation to teach more than is necessary. Trying to cram too much in is an all-too-common mistake. Most of us seem to have an unflagging desire to tell people everything we know. Our enthusiasm for our subject, coupled with guilt about short-changing our students, stops us from recognising the principles of good adult learning and teaching. At its most prosaic, it is far better for them to learn less rather better than more rather badly.

4   You may be working to an external syllabus and feel that you are compelled to teach it all. In fact there is more freedom to select and prioritise the content defined by a syllabus than would first appear, since they are as much guides as directives. Moreover, they rarely indicate the structure and emphases to be placed on particular topics nor do they usually specify the approach to be taken. If you have found out what your students already know and what they feel they need – their starting points – you will be able to identify what content is essential, what is peripheral and what is sufficiently well known for you not to devote too much time too it.

5   Not all the subject content that you think your students should engage with has to be presented within the session. Some of it will certainly lend itself to self-study or individual practice. Adults are responsible for their own learning, and they share with you the responsibility for the course. So negotiate with them the topics that they might follow up on their own rather than in course time. You will have to guide such 'distance learning' and help them decide whether their personal study can best be undertaken through the use of handouts, a work book, a reading plan or a practice schedule. However, resist the temptation of packing the spaces you create in your sessions with yet more content.

6   Many of the same points can be made about books which you may have selected as course texts. They are a learning resource rather than a teaching prescription. Even where you are using a commercial learning package – such as the sort the BBC produces so well for languages – you should select, re-order, reemphasise, and extend the material and accompanying exercises as seems best to you to meet the particular needs of your students.

7   The subject content of a given session does not have to be 'for all the people, all of the time'. This is what differentiation and personalised learning are about. Most groups consist of individuals with differing experiences, levels of expertise and

potential for learning. One of the advantages of organising participants into sub-groups is that you can choose the material each group is to work to match their needs more exactly. Watch out for the occasions when several students have much the same need, something that often happen in practical subjects where people are working on their own projects. Gathering an *ad hoc* group together will allow you to present some additional content or a refined technique more efficiently. By doing this you can satisfy those who cannot proceed any further without it, prepare others who will soon reach the stage where they will need it, without interrupting those who wouldn't benefit from such teaching at this point or who can already do it.

8   Many tutors lack confidence in their own knowledge and expertise. They spend hours studying everything they can lay their hands on in a desperate attempt to fill gaps in their knowledge and to find 'the ultimate answer' of what to teach. Keep up-to-date in your subject by all means, indeed you have a professional duty to do so, but focus less upon what you feel you don't know and more upon what your students actually *need* you to teach them.

KEY POINTS

- *Use the test 'need to know – nice to know' when deciding on what content to include.*
- *Prepare sufficient content, but if you teach rather less of it they may learn rather more.*

13 Constructing Course and Session Plans

There can be few teachers of adults who do not undertake some sort of preparation for their teaching, though each will approach the business of course and session planning in the ways they feel suit them best. Yet writing out a session plan is an end point, the culmination of a period of preparation and planning which will involve reading, reflection, discussion with students, selecting content, choosing appropriate methods, thinking through activities, anticipating group management issues, designing teaching aids, reviewing previous sessions and so on. Whatever labels you give the following elements, and however you document them, each has an important part to play in planning for learning and in subsequent teaching.

1 A *course title* is not without significance! As it is banner shorthand for what the course is about and even to whom it is directed, it needs to be inviting. Avoid ambiguity and use a sub-title and/or explanatory phrase where it helps. 'The psychology of little monsters' had less need of one than did 'Schubert: the man, his music and his legacy'. When the title of a poorly recruiting course was changed from 'The chemistry of naturally occurring alkaloids' to 'Plants that heal and kill' enrolments rocketed and attracted a huge a variety of people!

2 A *course outline, description, or syllabus* usually includes title, aims, learning outcomes, areas of content to be covered, level, group size, staffing, resources, timing, place, and venue. A paragraph setting out the context is also helpful. What a course description is *not* is a numbered list of topics. Write a draft outline at an early stage, then amend it to a final version once you have planned the course. If the primary readership is to be students, use an accessible, friendly style. Try 'you/we' instead of 'students' or the passive voice. Thus in a section about methods you might write: '... and in our study of these topics, we shall discuss some of the main issues together and work on others in small groups. We shall examine some facsimile documents,

maps and paintings and look at several sets of slides. There will be a number of handouts to help you keep a record of what we work on, and ...'

3   A *scheme of work*, or course running plan, lays out the material to be covered and how it will be approached session by session, though again, it could be worth while rethinking 'the obvious'. It may be that there are fundamental subject principles or skills which require that an order be followed, though there will almost certainly be topics that can be left until later. Think about including what people might enjoy doing during the early stages of a course that relates to what they already know ... or what they feel is at the heart of the subject ... or will give them a sense of achievement and a desire for more ... or that they can transfer to what they are doing elsewhere. This might produce an order that isn't 'the usual', though it may be one that will increase their motivation and learning.

   The methods you need to use to achieve particular learning outcomes may be incremental – though they may not. So also think about what beginners might *really* fancy doing that would motivate them to come back for more. Whilst there may be timing and resources constraints that you can't modify and formal assessment of student progress to be scheduled, still try to use a flexible approach that both meets the realities of being an adult student as well as the demands of the subject. A '20 topic, 20 weeks' approach, even for an accredited, assessed course, feels constrained and overly tutor determined. Amongst other things, it suggests a lack of awareness of how adults learn, the experience and learning they already possess, and the wisdom and experience they can contribute if you will allow them.

4   A *session plan* provides a working blueprint set out in a format which an individual tutor finds most useful. Amongst other things it should include aims, learning outcomes, content, methods, timing, and resources. Few tutors venture very far without such *aide-memoires* even if some still call it a *lesson* plan, a term reminiscent of schooling rather than working with adults.

Regardless of whether you are asked to submit your session plans or provide them for an OTL visit, they are your working document and you should be producing them for your own purposes. Select the items from the following list that seem useful and add any others that you think would be helpful. The more important ones are in **bold**.

- **date** and duration
- venue and room
- group description including indication of prior knowledge
- number in group + participant list
- room arrangement and seating plan
- session topic
- **session aim and learning outcomes**
- **session 'structure' showing timing, content** and **methods**
- **resources**
- **note of student achievements** and course evaluation
- **note of tutor's session evaluation**
- **note of what to do next**
- note of what to modify if this session is repeated.

5 There is no best way of setting out a session plan; the basic choice is between a timed sequence of notes of what is to be done and a table with column heading eg

- LOs + 7.30 ... 7.40 ... 8.10 ... etc
- timing + proposed LOs + content + methods + aids
- what the students are to do and why + what I am to do + what with + when
- a flow diagram showing: what>why>how>when

Whichever format you decide on, leave space to write in what was achieved during the session. Make a note of anything that went particularly well ... and less well, indicate anything that you would change another time and what you need to do next time. Do not delay doing it, hoping you will remember later: you won't, and your insights and your good ideas will be lost.

6   Some practical tips:

- Keep a separate course file for each of your courses. Store session plans sequentially using file dividers.

- If you find you need content reference notes – detailed factual material that you cannot carry in your head – write them down separately from the session plan. Make critical points stand off the page with highlight pens or underlining. Use a different coloured paper from the timed session plan so it is obvious which is which. If you use record cards, number them in case you drop them and/or punch a hole in one corner and tie them together with a loop of string or a treasury tag.

- Keep a copy of each handout you plan to use with your session plans. Write any management instructions on it clearly. Keep handout originals in transparent plastic folders: you may need more copies.

- Place any prepared A4 OHP acetate sheets in polythene plastic folders with a layer of plain paper between each. If you are using mounted OHP acetates, label and number them clearly.

7   It will be apparent that the relationship between a course outline, a scheme of work and a session plan is not only one of level – from the general to the specific – but also a dynamic one. It will be a most unusual session where everything goes according to plan. Most tutors find that they have to modify a session as it proceeds, taking into account unforeseen circumstances, modifying over-ambitious or too simplistic-plans and adapting to the pace of participants' learning and to their ongoing achievement (or lack of it). Moreover the outcomes of one session can and should influence the planning and conduct of the next and this in turn is likely to affect the scheme of work. The flow diagram (Illustration 5) tracks this interactive relationship.

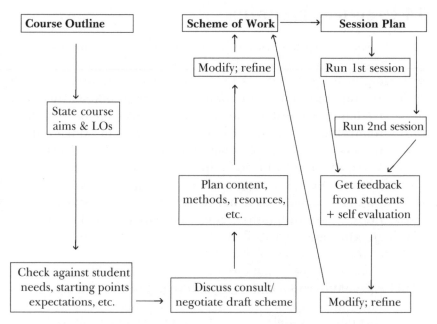

Illustration 5: Planning flow diagram

8   You should not expect that all your session aims or learning outcomes will be achieved just because you prepared carefully at the beginning. Planning for learning requires a flexible approach, continual modification and adaptation.

KEY POINTS

• *Take time and trouble in planning preparation; it will result in (much) better teaching and (much) more effective learning.*
• *Strike a balance between what people need, what they have already achieved, and the learning opportunities you can realistically provide for them.*

---

14 Practical Planning

This chapter is about the practical aspects of setting up a teaching course or training event from scratch. Circumstances will vary: you may have total responsibility for arranging a course and you have to do everything, or you don't have to but you still need to know what has been planned, that it has been done and that it accords with the ways you want to work. Which ever it is, 'come the day', you will have to deal with the problems that arise before they get in the way of people's learning and achievement. Your students will see it as 'down to you' to sort things out. Check through the following and highlight those aspects that *do* have a bearing on what you do and the circumstances in which you do it.

1   The preliminaries ... before you begin, find out about/agree ...

- the course's overall purpose(s) and any *required* learning outcomes
- the group – likely group (minimum and maximum)
- likely previous experience
- volunteers or 'required' attendance
- marketing
- enrolment procedures
- when you'll get the definitive list
- the training team if you are to work along side another tutor(s)
- any *required* content, methods, style, evaluation or assessment
- any *required* use of a pre-designed course
- the location, venue and available A/V resources
- any organisational and financial constraints
- time and timings
- the responsibility for bookings, material productions, ordering A/V equipment, etc.

2   Planning ... you must decide upon ...

- the detailed purpose(s)/aims of the course, and whether the course organiser has any covert ones

- what the learning outcomes are to be (and if you haven't written them, whether you subscribe to them and can work to them)
- up to date, correct and relevant content
- a progression within the course programme
- an appropriately paced 'scheme of work'
- the ways in which you will find out and then take account of the needs and starting points of students
- a variety of methods which will suit the material and participants' preferred ways of working and learning styles
- building in plenty of opportunities for participation and interaction
- potential flexibility within the programme to respond to the emergent needs of students
- the ways by which you and the students will know whether the learning outcomes have been achieved (ie assessment techniques)
- the transferability of achieved learning to participants' external activities
- whether you can work with a particular tutor if it is to be a team approach
- do you complement each other; do you think alike; do you share a similar style; share the same beliefs about adults and about the subject?

3   Setting it up ... and attention to detail about ...

- Location:
    - make a preliminary visit to check it all out
    - car parking; public transport
    - physical access to the venue
    - access for those with disabilities
    - sign posting ... and for your class/event
    - reception staff 'on duty', names and agreed responsibilities
    - requirements to lodge lists, timetables, etc

- Venue:
    - room location(s) and their proximity
    - heath and safety: especially fire escapes and risk assessment

- furniture (chairs, tables, orientation, arrangement)
- ventilation/heating
- light switches and power points
- blackout
- hearing loop
- proximity of lavatories

- Refreshments:
  - coffee (tea; decaf; fruit teas; juice; water)
  - quality biscuits, etc
  - meals (sit down; buffet; 'bring your own')
  - alternative dietary requirements
  - times and timing
  - who is to serve
  - where is it to be served

- Equipment:
  - flipchart stand and paper
  - fixed writing board
  - OHP and screen
  - PC + digital projector system
  - interactive board
  - video playback
  - video camera system
  - IT facilities
  - photocopying facilities
  - extension leads

- Materials:
  - handouts (preparation and printing)
  - name badges (readable from the front)
  - participants' files
  - spare paper, card, blank record cards
  - transparencies – dry copier and write-on
  - tutor's 'toolbox'

- Pre-course communication:
  - joining instructions

- map
- letter (personalised from you? from the organiser?)
- information about accommodation, dress, free time, time and timings, contact phone numbers
- pre-course tasks/requirements
- outline timetable, programme

4   On the day ... anticipate ...

- Getting there:
  - allow plenty of travel time
  - arrive *at the very least* 1 hour beforehand for a whole/half day event

- Venue staff:
  - introduce yourself
  - find out and use their names
  - agree any changes
  - provide final lists, timetables, etc
  - confirm times and timings
  - check refreshment arrangements
  - locate any extra facilities you may need
  - check for fire drills

- Venue:
  - (re)inspect teaching rooms
  - (re)check lights, plugs, blackout
  - check all the equipment (still) works
  - (re)arrange furniture
  - arrange resources/materials to hand

- Arrivals:
  - check/put up direction posters
  - set up registration location
  - confirm who is to register participants
  - set out participants' files, badges, etc

5   Running it ... make sure that you also ...

- Greet and meet:
  - wear a badge
  - welcome people personally
  - introduce yourself by name
  - use their names
  - smile
  - socialise

- Starting:
  - start on time
  - say 'Hello' and introduce yourself
  - state the fire regulations, exits and any H&S drills
  - do the *necessary* course descriptions & admin.
  - postpone most admin. matters until later
  - get started!

- Introductions:
  - use non-threatening introductory activities
  - small group work-related tasks are usually best
  - don't *waste* time on them
  - establish any confidentiality agreement
  - agree non discriminatory language/references

- Latecomers:
  - welcome them discretely
  - give them their files, missing materials, etc
  - help them to catch up
  - get them some coffee
  - ease them into working with a.n.other

- Atmosphere:
  - establish the equality of adulthood
  - treat them like adults
  - appear friendly, approachable, responsive and enthusiastic
  - create an atmosphere of informality and friendliness
  - encourage/facilitate interaction, participation and course ownership

- 'On course':
  - look for evidence of their engagement in the learning process
  - look for evidence of their learning gains
  - watch for cues and clues of course process strengths and weaknesses
  - consult with co-tutors if you want to modify things
  - explain, consult and negotiate with students about modifications
  - keep the room(s) tidy, especially at breaks
  - be last in any refreshment queues

- Ending:
  - summarise what you judge has been achieved
  - confirm any actions you have agreed to undertake
  - make a note of such actions and carry them out
  - thank people for coming and see them on their way
  - clear up and put the room back to some sort of order
  - thank the venue staff
  - agree an evaluation session with co-tutors
  - set a 'soonest' date or you will lose the benefit
  - be the last to leave

6 Evaluation ... and how to get the best from ...

- Procedure:
  - pencil and paper, avoiding simplistic ratings
  - small group + report back
  - large group open discussion
  - posted comments

- Timing:
  - timetable it as the penultimate activity
  - follow with a short, up-beat finale
  - secure commitment to any postal evaluation
  - provide stamped addressed envelopes

- Content:
  - seek judgements about the course and course process
  - seek judgements about learning outcome achievement
  - seek description/judgement of personal learning gains

- Feedback:
  - offer the group your evaluation before they leave
  - consider posting a synopsis of their assessments and evaluations

- Post course:
  - meet with co-tutors to review the course
  - review students' evaluations and assessments
  - assess overall learning gains – LOs and 'personal'
  - review your preparation, planning and management
  - review the location, venue, service and resources
  - review your working relationship with the organiser
  - identify course process strengths and weakness
  - identify what you need to modify/confirm for next time
  - identify future training needs and progression
  - reflect upon your own 'performance'
  - share/confirm/sensitively challenge co-tutors' performance
  - write a report for the organiser/organisation
  - construct a synopsis for participants and send it.

KEY POINTS

- *Think 'what would I want as a course member?'*
- *You will have to cope with any crises that arise, so prevent them from even happening by thorough preparation.*

III Methods

Introduction

Whilst the term 'teaching method' can readily be understood to mean a procedure chosen to teach something to someone, the meaning of 'learning method' is less clear. It may refer to a teaching method viewed from a learner's perspective but it can also be used to denote the subjective activity involved, ie rote learning, trial and error learning, discovery learning, and so on. We have decided to use the less ambiguous term 'methods', taking it to mean any designed or planned opportunity for adult learning which involves some form of direct or indirect choice and management by a tutor.

This section considers the choice and management of methods, working with large and small groups, resources and audio visual aids, and the devising of tasks and activities.

15 Categorising and Choosing Methods

There can be no universal method suitable for all events and for all people. The preferences which different people have for acquiring and processing information strongly suggests that a variety of methods are needed to provide them with a range of alternative ways to learn. A choice of activities – listening, looking, talking, doing – has the potential to give each adult the time and opportunity to extract meaning, draw comparisons, recognise and connect the new with what s/he already knows in the ways that s/he prefers to learn.

1   A useful starting point for making choices between methods is to group them according to type of activity:

   – *presentation* – where the tutor predominantly transmits ideas, information or skills eg by lecturing or demonstrating
   – *interaction* – where knowledge and experience are shared between the tutor and the students and/or amongst the students themselves eg by discussion, questioning or role play
   – *self-enquiry* (also called *search*) – where students work on their own, though they may do so in concert with others, exploring and discovering for themselves, eg by individual practice, reading or completing a project or assignment.

   This is a better categorisation than the learner centred/teacher centred dichotomy which often carries the assumption that the former is ethically and psychologically superior to the latter.

2   Another helpful category is by the domain of learning, where methods are grouped according to the content to which they are best suited:

   – the *affective* domain – concerned with attitudes, where appropriate methods include discussion, case study, and role play
   – the *psycho motor* domain – concerned with skills, where

appropriate methods include demonstration, individual
practice with supervision
- the *cognitive* domain – concerned with knowledge, where appropriate methods include lectures, project work and questioning.

3   When you set about choosing a method, ask yourself the
question: 'Is this the method which will best help these adults
acquire that planned learning outcome(s) in those
circumstances?' Decide which predisposing factors are relevant,
asking yourself whether the method sits happily with:

- the subject content/type of material
- the proposed learning outcomes
- the need for change of activity
- the group size, and student familiarity with a method
- the preferred ways of learning and any special needs of
  individuals your experience and management skills of that
  method the resources and facilities available.

4   It may be that one or more of these factors are so compelling
that a first choice is less appropriate for the particular group
and circumstance you have in mind, and there is a better
alternative. You can choose from:

Brainstorming	**Individual practice and supervision**
Buzz group	Lecture/talk
Carousel	**Lecture/talk with participation**
Case study	Questioning Socratic questioning
Continuum ranking	Rainbowing
Contract making	Role play
Debate; Panel; Witness	Seminar
Demonstration	Simulation
Diary; log	**Small group work**
Directed reading	Snowballing
Discussion	Tutorials/private interview
Games	Visit; Field trip
Goldfish bowl	Projects/assignment
Icebreakers	

... where the items in **bold** are the major methods for working with adults. The following chapter on managing methods [16] describes all of the above in turn and gives some management guidelines for each.

KEY POINTS

- *Look for the method which will best help most participants learn and achieve more of the time.*
- *Extend the range of methods you use ... it is good for your professional development as well as your students' learning.*

---

16 Managing Methods

Each of the methods described below have been labeled with the activity and the domain categories, and the optimum group size. The term 'plenary group' means an undivided teaching group, and 'small group' includes subdivided groups of 2–6.

BRAINSTORMING (interactive; cognitive and affective; plenary)

Brainstorming (also known as First Thoughts) – *a free, spontaneous listing of group participants' responses to a theme or topic* – identifies the alternative ideas and/or opinions within a group. The resulting list is used as the basis for a subsequent task or discussion.

1   The theme should be clear and unambiguous. Write it at the top of the flipchart, white board or OHP acetate as well as telling the group what you have in mind. Make sure students are aware of the sort of responses you are seeking – synonyms, feelings, associations, etc – and whether you want one word, a phrase or a sentence.

2   Encourage people to produce ideas quickly: it should be a fun activity, so keep up the momentum. Set a time-limit. Write up each comment without judgment or interpretation, though acknowledge the person who has offered it. You may edit a contribution by shortening it or using a paraphrase as long as you check that what you propose to write up is what was meant. (If you use a scribe from the group, be sure s/he writes down the agreed contribution.)

3   Handling and making sense of the ideas once they have been offered can sometimes be difficulty. It is a good idea to work out the likely categories of responses beforehand, then sectionalise the flip chart (actually, or in your head) and write each contribution in the appropriate category. You might use two or even three flip chart sheets fixed to the wall. This way you can

understand and handle the groups of suggestions that have been made much more easily. 'So let's first look at these which all have to do with ...'

4 Ensure that you make subsequent use of what has been listed, perhaps as a trigger for discussion or as a link to the next section. Consider whether it would be useful to reproduce the sheet as a handout, especially if you want to return to it at a later date. If you do, hang on to the original sheet too.

BUZZ GROUP (interactive; cognitive and affective; plenary)

A buzz group – *a brief informal discussion of a question or short topic between pairs or trios* – promotes participation, shares individual impressions, creates a focus and can change the immediate focus of a session.

1 A buzz group is a useful and quick way to involve people. As it is short, informal and requires a minimum of setting up, it can be repeated more than once in a session. Keep the questions or problems you pose simple – 'What are the perennial news items that have always sold newspapers?' ... 'Why shouldn't you jump in when you see someone drowning?'

2 When you set up buzz groups, make it clear who students should work with eg 'the person sitting next to you ... behind you ... who you haven't spoken with today', and that they know who their partner(s) is before you say what you want them to discuss. Check – again – that everyone knows what you want them to do and how long they have.

3 The need for good management notwithstanding, make the whole activity punchy. If you use buzz groups on a second or third occasion during a session ask people to work with a different partner. If you use the method for no other reason than to give the group chance to change sitting positions and refocus their attention, it would still be worthwhile in terms of their comfort and preventing 'micro-sleeps'.

4   Use informal feedback to gauge the flavour of what they have been talking about. Ask a couple of pairs for their response, or get two or three people to call out one point each and then build upon their suggestions. Buzz groups are about directing attention and arousing interest rather than problem solving *per se*.

CAROUSEL (interactive; cognitive and affective; plenary)

A carousel – *a timed sequence of integrated pair work whereby an individual engages with a number of partners in a two-ringed musical chairs arrangement* – provides varied experiences of people's responses to the same issue, and can build up the views and opinions of a group to different aspects of one or more issues.

1   Arrange an even number of chairs in two concentric circles such that pairs of chairs face each other. Divide the group into two – inner and outer – and seat them opposite each other in the two circles. The change in partners is effected by the outer circle moving to their left (or right). If you have a large plenary group and sufficient space, run two carousels at the same time though watch for incipient chaos!

2   Explain the task clearly, preferably with the instructions/questions on a handout, especially if the task is to vary as each new pair meets. State the time to be allowed for each dialogue and start the first one off. Move the outer circle 1, 2 or 3 places at 'time', regardless of whether everyone has finished. (If, after the first exchange, you see that your timing is awry, announce the change of timing for succeeding dialogues.)

3   If you have an odd number of students, select an observant individual from the group to watch what takes place. Ask him/her to give a verbal report at the end. (If *you* make up the numbers you won't be able to manage the activity or the timing properly.)

4   Once the carousel is complete, give people a breather as they are likely to be quite excited. Collect in some feedback by asking

for the findings from one or two inner and outer participants. Ask your observer to give a report and invite other comments from both circles to elucidate or add to what s/he says. Build upon what has been learned and/or revealed in what you do next.

CASE STUDY (interactive and self-enquiry; cognitive and affective; small group and individual)

A case study – *a history or set of circumstances of some event in written/ visual format for group study and discussion* – provides real-life situations for group analysis whereby individuals can try out ideas and solutions with others, free from direct emotional involvement and real time constraint. Case studies develop the ability to identify underlying principles and processes, test current learning and facilitate transfer.

1   It is all too easy to be seduced by well-written and entertaining material which subsequently proves to be at the wrong level, either because the solution is too obvious or because it is beyond students' experience or current interpretive powers. Case study material must relate to the planned learning outcomes. If appropriate cases are not ready to hand, construct your own. Allow plenty of time to write them and trial each one on someone who will give you an honest opinion. Good material should encapsulate the important features without too much detail and allow for the possibility of differing interpretations, thus encouraging discussion and subsequent learning and transfer.

2   There are alternatives to descriptive text. You can, for example, create case material as a series of letters and memos. Alternatively, you could photocopy anonymous photographs, attach invented details and pose a dilemma, or use newspaper articles with other real or concocted documentary evidence to create an issue to be resolved. You could develop a case study with the group, first guiding them towards the underpinning features you think are required, and then asking them to solve it. Small groups could create case studies for other groups to work on 'whilst we work on their case'.

3   Small group work is likely to be the most appropriate way of organising case studies. At some stage let everyone know the bones of the other cases being discussed even if they are not to work on them. At the end, let them hear the interpretations of those who did. Give them the scripts and the appropriate interpretations as a handout later. Expect that students *will* want to know what the solution is, even though you judge that it is the working on the problems that is important. Work out your analyses beforehand and be prepared to say what you think (or know) *are* likely answers and why. Make sure you draw out the principles and transferable skills.

CONTINUUM RANKING (interactive; all domains; plenary)

Continuum ranking – *simple comparative decisions-making using physical interaction and movement* – provides an immediate physical picture of the group's attributes and/or views, and promotes group interaction.

1   Continuum ranking usually uses a linear arrangement, so you can suggest an imaginary line with the extremes at either end, draw a real line with chalk or unravel a ball of string. Participants are asked to place themselves along the continuum by age, by strength of attitude or opinion, by level of aptitude or skill, etc. In order to do so they must engage with other members of the group. Thereafter you can ask them to discuss why they have positioned themselves as they have, and/or to reposition themselves according to 'where you were a year ago' or 'where you would like to be'.

2   You can also make use of a two-dimensional arrangement whereby individuals rate themselves on two attributes eg home and the course location by direction and by distance, or radical/ reactionary views by tough/tender minded behaviour.

3   This method requires space so you may need to rearrange the room. Where you use it during a session rather than as the initial

activity, ask people to gather up their belongings and chairs and move them well out of the way. To avoid having them standing around feeling awkward, explain what you want them to do and how you want them to do it *before* you ask them to get up. Once everything is ready, remind them again of who goes where and what they are to do. Manage each stage and make sure that everyone is listening as you move them on to any new specification.

4 Ranking can be used to promote group interaction, ie as an icebreaker, as well as a basis for discussion and/or subsequent investigation. Ensure that you are clear why you wish to use it, for though it is likely to be fun, it can become banal unless you have a worthwhile learning outcome. If you feel you can, use the information it provides to make occasional and gentle reference later in the course to some of the quirky details people may have revealed.

CONTRACT MAKING (interactive and self-enquiry; all domains; small group and individual)

Contract making or action planning – *individuals setting up a personal undertaking or plan of action* – promotes self-awareness and reflection of strengths and shortcomings, identifies appropriate development whilst motivating and committing an individual to a course of action that can be practiced and achieved.

1 This method requires everyone's commitment not only to engage in the process but to carry out the proposed behaviour. Before you begin, discuss with people the potential learning outcomes, the procedure involved and the likely requirements to be made of them beyond the course. Each needs to feel willingly contracted to work towards the goals that s/he has set for him/herself.

2 Having negotiated the method with the whole group, allow students to choose their own small groups of two or three unless you have specific reasons for requiring them to do otherwise. Remind them that they should begin by analysing each

individual's present level of knowledge or skill and then move on to identify what that person hopes to achieve and the circumstances in which s/he might do so. Partners should facilitate and support each other in arriving at their individual plans of action. Provide a handout. One way is to have spaces for: 'I can do *X* ... and ... I want to be able do *Y*. I will try to achieve *Y* in this way ... in these circumstances ... to this level ... in that time scale ... and I talked to *A* and *B* about it'. Ensure the self-contract sheets are completed for later reference. Monitor the groups and offer guidance where necessary.

3   It may be inappropriate to ask people to share all of their proposals with the plenary group at this stage, but you could summarise the sort of things people have proposed. End the session by saying what you think has been achieved and to what they are committed.

4   If people are meeting at a later date, reinstate the small groups and ask them to review the outcomes of what they have attempted. An alternative procedure is to make a copy of each action plan, then post it to the individual concerned after an appropriate period with a note asking 'what happened ... and when ... and how ... and with what overall result?'

DEBATE; PANEL; EXPERT WITNESS (presentational and interactive; cognitive and affective; plenary)

Debates and panels – *public events adapted to teaching and learning purposes* – provide the opportunity to listen to and discuss topics of interest with specialists. They allow first hand contact with those directly engaged within a subject, and the ideas and practices involved.

1   Brief all members of a panel or debating team, what is expected of them, what levels of analysis, explanation and discussion are appropriate, and who the students are. Any topic chosen should have valid arguments for and against, and debate/panel members should reflect such diversity. Chair the event yourself as you

will know the students, their strengths, weaknesses and knowledge base, and can mediate and extend the discussion to best advantage.

2   Make sure that the group is prepared and that people have some background knowledge to make best use of the ideas and opinions they may hear. Questions for a panel can be prepared in advance and you might review them, offering suggestions and amendments as appropriate. Give the event a social flavour; arrange for the group to socialize with the visitors afterwards so that they can follow up items of interest.

3   Unlike a guest speaker, the brief of an Expert Witness is to provide answers to direct questions from the group as in a law court, though s/he may give a brief introduction to establish his/her areas of expertise and fields of interest. A witness will need to be well briefed about what is needed by the group and their levels of current understanding. If s/he is not an experienced group facilitator, you may need to chair the session. Expert witnesses can be summoned to open up or move on a long-term project.

4   Panels and debates are good vehicles for developing ideas and understanding within the group itself. They can be organised with students as panelists, and proposing/opposing a motion. There may be individuals in the group who have areas of expertise which would equip them to act as expert witnesses. Take care that the quieter and less articulate students are not ignored, and you encourage everyone to play a part.

DEMONSTRATION (presentational; psycho motor; plenary)

A demonstration – *a formal/informal display which provides a model of how to do something, usually divided into key stages and accompanied by an explanatory commentary* – can be either *Watch me first* or *Do it with me*. It is ideally followed by supervised individual practice.

1   Be clear exactly what you are going to demonstrate, and why, and that you yourself can do it adequately. Bear in mind that what is easy and obvious to you may not be to students and that an over-slick demonstration may rob people of their self-confidence when they come to practice it themselves.

2   Check that everyone can see and hear. Have people grouped close by so that you can show them the intricacies of what you are doing. If some have to be at a distance because you need to show a major physical activity, you could use a raised position – a dais, stage or table. Speak clearly and distinctly and make eye contact with people.

3   Before you begin the demonstration describe what you intend to do, how and why. 'Show and tell' the finished product or run through the complete activity first so that they know what they are aiming for. Letting the group see the entirety at the start will help them visualise and build each component into a meaningful whole: the *Blue Peter* technique – 'and here's one I've made earlier' – has *much* to recommend it. If you can only do the thing once – because you only have a single set of ingredients or materials – describe the steps you will take, perhaps miming the crucial actions and/or holding up the components. Diagrams and models may well be helpful, but make them much bigger than life size so that the stitches, or joints, or folds, or whatever, are abundantly clear.

4   Accompany each step of the demonstration with a verbal description. Your words should marry your actions though you do not have to talk all the time or give a continuous running commentary. More involved manoeuvres might be best completed in silence. Language is important so use words that everyone will understand. Nevertheless, it can be a good opportunity to introduce technical terms since you will be able explain or show what new words relate to. (Write them down on a flipchart.) Encourage students to ask questions about the process – and the product – as you are demonstrating. If you need to delay an answer for a minute whilst you complete some

action they will understand. Take care to pace the demonstration and remember that when you are facing people, your left and right will appear reversed. Think knot tying or knitting!

5   Give out any instructional handouts at the appropriate times. There is no best practice 'before or after' rule. Include any new technical terms you have introduced.

6   Once you have finished demonstrating, check the process has been fully grasped. Ask if there are any points that students are not sure about and whether they would like you to go over anything a second time. Offer to repeat the process if it makes sense to do so. Alternatively, ask people to check with one another that they know what to do by showing each other or talking it through. Individuals may in fact have missed a point and feel happier about asking a colleague than admitting it in front of the group.

7   End the demonstration with an informal discussion to review what the group thinks they will find easy or hard, fun or impossible! The chances are that you didn't find it *that* easy when you first started either, so tell them how it was for you. Distribute any printed material or handouts setting out the main points if you have not already done so, and finish with a word of encouragement to motivate individuals to start work on their own.

8   Your observation and assessment of students' attempts to carry out the activity you have just demonstrated is the best test of whether they have understood. On the basis of what you see them do, you can assess their proficiency and modify what you do next. You may judge that you need to repeat the demonstration (or some part of it) so that everyone has grasped the point. Alternatively, you could invite a competent member of the group to demonstrate whilst you comment upon what she/he is doing. Choose carefully and take care not to embarrass an individual or set up any competition within the group.

DIARY; LOG (self-enquiry; all domains; individual)

A diary – *a personalised record of progress, development and reactions to work achieved and/or to the process of the course* – helps individuals keep track of their progress, practice and responses, and/or particular themes and issues.

1   The benefits of keeping a diary include developing self-awareness and self-assessment skills as well as recording evidence of behaviour. Kept and reviewed, it can show the change and development that have taken place over time. However, for these to become apparent, you will need to confirm that what participants are recording includes analysis and does not remain purely descriptive.

2   Maintaining diary entries is a problem. If you continually remind people and/or have to provide course time for completion, the process can become onerous. Conversely, if you fail to mention it at all, few may bother to keep their entries up to date. Once you have established with the group the purposes of a learning diary and secured their willingness to keep one, negotiate with them as to how best they can be helped to maintain it. Agree their rights of confidentiality and privacy, whilst deciding how you together can make use of what they are writing. If you plan to review people's diaries regularly, be aware that you will alter what they write, especially if any assessment is involved.

3   An alternative to asking people to maintain a written diary is to encourage them to collect sketches, pictures, quotations, newspaper articles and other ephemeral items. Suggest that these items be pasted into an A4 exercise book or file and commented on using balloon captions. Such a document becomes a personal log or portfolio, and entries can be made as needed rather than on a strictly session by session basis. It is likely to prove more fun and people may be more motivated to maintain it, enjoy doing it and make more practical use of what they produce. You might also suggest they keep a web log!

4   Consider the possibility of small groups keeping a shared diary, or, indeed, a single diary/scrap book by and for the whole group. You would need to devote course time to it however, and negotiate your involvement when it is to be discussed and/or filled-in.

DIRECTED READING (self-enquiry; cognitive and affective; individual)

Directed reading –*focused private study* – draws attention to particular aspects, develops thought and confirms/extends knowledge and understanding.

1   Where a session depends upon the group being familiar with a section of text, set the expectation that it has to be done by everyone. The amount that you ask them to do should be less rather than more, essential rather than peripheral, occasional rather than regular. You should confirm people's ability and willingness to do it, especially if they are part-time.

2   The material itself must be accessible. It is unlikely that a library will hold multiple copies, so photocopy the appropriate sections if the material is not part of a course set book. (Be sure that you are covered by an institution's copyright license.) Consider making up a selected reader which is loaned to participants.

3   Ensure that you know the material yourself, that it actually does contain what you think it contains, and the task you have set is possible. Provide written guidelines of what you want people to take into account. Give prompt questions to help people comprehend and assimilate what they are reading. Suggest that they might write a critique.

4   Acknowledge that people have done the activity and use the material that has been studied by making direct and indirect references to it. Where people see that it doesn't seem to matter whether they read what you ask or not, they will cease to do so. Decide how you are going to cope with those who haven't done

the reading. If there is only a couple, you could continue with the planned follow-up discussion asking them to listen in. If, on the other hand, rather few have done the reading, then you will need to give a quick guided tour of the piece and work on from there. In this latter situation, check with the group whether it is worth persevering with assigned reading if it is causing difficulties for so many.

5   When you offer a list of books to be read, make it very short and annotate it. Note whether a book is essential, background, up-to-date and well-written. Offer a short synopsis of the important titles and say where they can be obtained and at what cost; provide bibliographical details and the availability of photocopies.

DISCUSSION (interactive; cognitive and affective; plenary)

A discussion – *a managed, interpersonal and cooperative exploration of a topic* – shares knowledge, ideas, opinions and attitudes. It can be effective in modifying attitudes, developing self-confidence, communication skills and critical reasoning.

1   Group discussion promotes learning and attitude change, though without a core of received knowledge, it can degenerate into pooled ignorance. Determine the learning outcomes of the discussion and agree them with the group plus anything else that you hope they may get out of it. It is helpful to identify the topic to be discussed sometime before and to guide people's pre-reading/thinking to the point where they can participate to some purpose. Even if the discussion is to follow straight on from a video, pre-session reading, a demonstration, a talk, or small group work, design some lead-in questions to give an initial structure to the discussion.

2   The size of a discussion group needs to be large enough to include a variety of opinions and experience, whilst still allowing each individual to feel that they can contribute safely. Divide a plenary group much larger than twenty into two: smaller

numbers in a discussion group will encourage the less confident and draw upon everyone's viewpoint. As you will need to monitor both groups, choose a chair/facilitator for each group who will be able to do the job effectively. Brief them beforehand about what you hope will be achieved. Recombine the groups later, ask for a summary of their main ideas and opinions, and draw some conclusions.

3   Arrange the environment to facilitate the dialogue; remove any tables and place the chairs into a circle with gaps to let people get in and out. Seat everyone without their sitting (or hiding) behind each other. Try to avoid cliques sitting next to each other and old antagonists sitting opposite each other. There is no optimum time period for a discussion: when you prepare the session, decide how much time you can devote to it bearing in mind the topic, the group, and whether all the learning outcomes seem achievable.

4   You will need to manage what goes on. Be aware that some adults may not find it easy to join in open group discussions. You will need to offer sympathetic encouragement and support to quieter individuals to help them participate. Make selective use of questions. It might be useful to ask what they *feel* about something rather than what they *think* as this will seem less threatening. Do not pressurise anyone, but make it clear that you and the rest of the group are interested in hearing everyone's contribution. Silences do not have to be filled immediately. People need time to reflect upon what has just been said and to decide how to respond.

5   Encourage people to treat each other's viewpoints with respect, even though they may disagree with some of the ideas expressed or attitudes held. If you – or they – show violent disapproval of someone's position, a whole section of the group could be alienated. On the other hand, you should challenge statements which display ageist, sexist and other discriminatory attitudes. Be sensitive in the ways you handle the over-talkative members. Make it clear that you value their opinions but you would also like to hear from other people. If necessary, have a gentle word with them at a coffee break.

6 Keep the group focused. Clarify vague or confusing remarks by querying obvious misconceptions and wrong ideas if others do not. You may need to check that everyone understands what is being said. Ask contributors to substantiate statements, especially if they seem prejudicial or are displaying rigid attitudes.

7 Discussions can fade, though on occasion people become so enthusiastic and interested it is difficult to stop them. Call a halt at a natural break in the discussion, no later than the time you have decided to stop, though cut it short if it's flagging. Summarise what has been discussed, review the main points and indicate how it is to be made use of. (You might also make a written summary and offer it as a handout. One person in the group might be willing to do this if you have agreed it beforehand.) Thank people for having taken part. Find time to speak to anyone who has made a particularly useful contribution, or who has participated for the first time, or who has seemed unusually quiet.

GAMES (interactive; cognitive and psycho motor; small group)

Educational games – *formalised games which simplify real-life situations by isolating particular skills, relationships or activities* – encourage inductive and deductive thinking, facilitate problem solving, decision making and team work, and can link practice to theory.

1 Educational games may be commercially produced or 'home grown'. They typically involve some degree of chance and can be based upon a board and dice, cards, or a set of prescribed circumstances. Properly designed games, introduced and handled in the right way, can encourage group interaction and help people learn by simulated doing. Make sure that there is a good match of fitness to purpose. There is a fine line between adult involvement and enjoyment in a worthwhile activity and a patronising, childish frolic. Some adults may not take to overly competitive games or feel that the subject is too serious to be treated flippantly by a mere game.

2   Review any commercial educational game and ensure that it will meet the learning outcomes you have in mind and that it is at the right level. Make sure you know the rules; play it yourself to discover any inherent problems and to establish the time it takes to complete. If you are making your own game, be aware that designing, piloting and amending is a lengthy business after which you may still need to mass produce items for the use of several small groups at once. Wherever it comes from, it should work, be enjoyable to play and people should learn something from it.

3   Positioning of a game within the session so that it acts as a novel change from the preceding activities. When you introduce the game, specify its purpose, the time required, the rules to be used and that you are the final arbiter! (If the game has a covert outcome – eg team building or leadership – you must explain to the group afterwards why you used a degree of subterfuge and didn't fully inform them at the beginning. If you think that this might cause difficulties, don't use it.)

4   Educational games should be fun and enjoyable but they should also be followed by time looking at what has been learnt. Help people identify the message the game contained, the implicit principle(s), how what they have learnt relates to their existing knowledge, and how it can transfer to future practice.

GOLDFISH BOWL (interactive; all domains; plenary)

Goldfish bowl – *a plenary group observation of a small group action* – allows participants to observe, analyse and evaluate the actions/ behaviour of others, and/or assume their roles to further some action.

1   The general procedure is for two or more of the group to discuss something, perform a task, or act out a role play whilst everyone else sits or stands round them, observing and taking note of the ideas, implied intentions, and/or skills being displayed. The observed pair can remain the same throughout or they can be replaced during/at the end of a scene according to a prearranged schedule.

2   Decide why this rather public (and potentially threatening) activity is more appropriate than small groups working with only one or two observers. It may be that a particular group of participants have something to offer the rest and this is the best way in which to do it, or that you judge there is merit in the group observing some members – or every member – doing something. There may be value in playing tag whereby people take up some procedure where others leave off with any differences being observed and commented on.

3   Introduce the idea of a goldfish bowl with care, clarify the purpose(s) with the group and confirm that they are willing to be involved. Since it requires a small group of individuals doing something whilst being observed by the rest, there may be some reticence, at least in the early stages. Ensure you have genuine volunteers to start the ball rolling. Legitimise anyone opting-out at any stage, though if they do, their subsequent contributions to the follow up discussion will need to be reconsidered.

4   Identify who is to begin inside the bowl, what the observers are to observe, and whether anyone is to take over part-way through. Check (again) that those in the bowl are at ease with what they are to do and that subsequently they aren't struggling to achieve something that they find is beyond them. Once the action is complete, work with the group to determine what has been learnt both by players and observers, and how this new knowledge and understanding can be used and/or transferred.

ICEBREAKERS (interactive; affective; plenary)

Icebreakers – *simple social group gaming techniques* – promote integration of individuals and help a group to gel.

1   Though icebreaker activities play a useful role in establishing a relaxed and cooperative atmosphere, they need to be used with caution. People new to such methods may be startled by them, especially if they have had no prior warning. Unless you are

sure that the circumstances are entirely appropriate and/or people are familiar with their use, it would be wise to avoid using involved icebreakers altogether.

2   Make it clear to the group what you are asking them to do and why. Avoid requiring them to do anything that will make them feel awkward or embarrassed. This includes standing up too soon or starting when they are still unsure of what or with whom it is to be done, let alone some of the more complicated icebreaking procedures.

3   Some activities include:
    –   ask for a show of hands for particular attributes/experience
    –   go round the group with people saying who they are, where they're from, why they have come, their likes/dislikes, etc
    –   pairs introduce each other after a short conversation
    –   you provide a list of names and people find out who's who and something about each other
    –   continuum ranking
    –   ask people to write 3 or 4 non obvious facts about themselves on unnamed cards which are collected and shuffled; individuals have to match the dealt card with the person
    –   round the group introductions except that after saying his/her name, the speaker repeats all the names of those preceding him/her. Make sure the group knows that you will be the last to do it!
    –   round the group introductions then introduce a soft bean bag or similar. The first person says his/her own name and then the name of person to whom they are throwing it, and so on.

4   If you decide that only simple introductions are appropriate, use some small group activities early on in the session, changing the group compositions each time. The interaction which results from working on a real task will help people feel at ease, more self-confident, and serve more purposes than a purely social icebreaker may do.

INDIVIDUAL PRACTICE WITH SUPERVISION (interactive
and self-enquiry; cognitive and psycho motor; individual)

Individual practice with supervision – *a monitored opportunity for
students to acquire and/or practice a skill within a managed environment
with the provision of feedback* – provides the necessary support and
resources to enable people to practice and develop a skill.

1   Unless individual practice as a whole group is the norm, warn
    people beforehand so that they can come properly prepared.
    Even where the practice follows directly on a demonstration
    you should specify clearly what you want or expect individuals
    to do. Ensure that everyone is employing the correct procedure
    from the start. You may decide that you are going to shape their
    actions from an approximation to a finished product, but it is
    sometimes difficult to correct over-learnt mistakes once an
    individual feels s/he is well on the way to success. Where it is a
    whole group activity, inject enthusiasm and fun into the
    proceedings and emphasise the benefits that can and should
    accrue. Warn the group that they may not do it perfectly first
    time but that everyone should make some progress. Organise
    things so that the opportunity for competition is minimal for
    there may be some who want to be obviously 'best' (and you
    should have a private word with them later).

2   Observe and listen to each person in order to diagnose what s/
    he is doing. Make an assessment in terms of his/her previous
    performance, the nature and difficulty of the new activity, and
    what you judge him/her to be capable of at this stage. Find out
    what the individual thinks about what s/he's doing and praise
    him/her for trying as well as achieving. Give specific suggestions
    rather than vague assurances. Encourage each individual,
    making sure that the quality of performance that is being aimed
    for is within his/her capacity.

3   Allocate your time fairly between individuals. Adults will not expect equal time from you every session but they will expect you to be fair overall. Guard against giving too much attention to the pushy individual, or the good one, or the least able, at the expense of the rest. Be conscious of the group as a whole, even as you are dealing with one person. Listen and watch for those who are bored, mystified or ready for more. If you see or hear that others want your assistance, acknowledge their requests and indicate that you will get to them and how long it might be until you can. There is no reason why an individual shouldn't seek immediate help from someone else who can do it, but make sure s/he doesn't become a nuisance.

4   *Coaching* involves more intensive 1:1 contact between smaller numbers of individuals and a tutor/trainer, and it includes more direct individualised instruction both before and during the period of practice. It also has to do with careful observation, analysis, and feedback to an individual about his/her ongoing performance.

5   The purpose of practicing any activity is for the individual to be able do it more efficiently and effectively. When adults experience positive results and achieve something they see to be worthwhile, they will act more independently and their own achievement will spur them to further success. Until then, they are more dependent and you will need to provide the reinforcement. But wherever they are, offer positive feedback, constructive criticism and affirmation.

6   There are at least 37 ways of saying 'Good' that you might use:

1	I like that!	8	Terrific!
2	That's right!	9	Good work!
3	That's the way!	10	*That's* better!
4	You're doing fine!	11	Excellent!
5	Nice going!	12	Good going!
6	Superb!	14	Smashing!
7	That's great!	15	That's really nice!

16	That's good work!	26	That's better than ever!
17	Much better!	27	Well done!
18	Splendid!	28	Now that is good!
19	That's first class!	29	Good for you!
20	That's coming along nicely!	30	You've cracked it!
21	You're doing that beautifully!	32	You did that very well!
		33	Tremendous!
22	That's it!	34	I *do* like that!
23	That's good!	35	Great!
24	You must be really pleased	36	Keep it up!
25	You are doing really well!	37	Wow!

7   In a number of subjects, especially ICT and craft subjects, a major amount of students' time is spent working on their own, perhaps using a study manual, computer programme or an individual creative project. Consequently a high proportion the session will involve you going round and working with individuals. Whilst much of what has already been said remains relevant, there are some additional features of this more intense 'circular tour' way of working that are worth stating. The particular advantages of 1:1 are that each student's learning progress and achievement can be assessed more precisely, and tailored responses can be offered to confirm what s/he can already do, to move him/her on in the right direction, and to offer specific help and guidance in ways that s/he will find most helpful.

8   You may be working with an individual student for one several reasons – s/he has asked for your help; you may have seen s/he is in need of some guidance, support or encouragement; you feel you need to intervene for some control or disciplinary reason; you want to make some ongoing or formal assessment of progress; it is his/her turn.

9   Decide where you are going to position yourself; you could appear threatening if you stand behind and speak over the person's head. S/he cannot see your expression and you cannot make eye contact, both important features of communication.

Exactly what you do depends upon how long you need to be with him/her. For a short visit you might crouch down or lean from the side, whilst it would be worth pulling up a chair for a longer stay. Although you will both spend much of your time looking at his/her work or VDU and keyboard, make sure that you do look at the student from time to time, try to make regular eye contact ... and don't forget to smile.

10 Expect to begin the discussion with an informal greeting, using the student's name early on and making it clear why you are there. 'So, Chris, sorry to keep you waiting ... what's the problem ... how can I help? I saw you were looking a bit perplexed ... I noticed you were chatting to Parveen ... have you come to a full stop?' Take care to keep your voice at a quiet and confidential level.

– Give the student time and space to explain the problem or tell you where they are up to. Resist jumping in too quickly with a solution, even if it is immediately obvious to you and you want to get on. Observe and listen first, diagnose second, respond last.

– Whilst your first inclination may be to take over and solve the difficulty, hold back. It is unlikely that your student will learn very effectively from your sleight of hand. Similarly, avoid launching into a verbal explanation which, whilst quite correct and comprehensible to another expert, may leave the student utterly confused.

– When you work with an individual think first about his/her levels of competence and understanding and then decide how you are going to help. Will it be enough to remind him/her of something s/he has already done successfully? Will you need to give a fuller explanation or will you first have to demonstrate, and then take him/her through it step by step? (There may well be a case for bringing the class together to work through a particular issue where several may be struggling and/or be likely to meet the same problem shortly.)

– Which ever procedure you use – and it will depend on individual need – adjust your level of explanation and your language to suit the student. However obvious a solution might seem to you, take care how you talk about it. S/he may already be feeling frustrated and foolish that s/he's unable to do it – s/he will not want to be additionally confused!

11 Where possible, let the student carry out the actions him/herself once s/he understands what is to be done, or how to start if you are providing step by step instructions. Such active learning by the student will prove the most effective. Before you leave, check that s/he has understood how, where or why the initial problem arose and that s/he now knows how to handle a similar problem next time. If you are in any doubt, ask the student to tell you what s/he has just done: 'Just take me through how to do X again'. Confirm that s/he knows what to go on to next and how to proceed thereafter.

12 Where you are carrying out some progress check or making a routine visit, use the same 'Hello + name' procedure, before adding: 'I've come to see how you are getting on', or some such. It is quite likely that what you can see will confirm his/her progress but you should still ask something like: 'How far have you got/getting on? ... have you managed to do X?' Check that s/he has arrived at the particular stage by an optimum procedure and make sure that s/he understands what s/he's doing. If you think it appropriate to offer some additional guidance or alter his/her existing way of doing something, do it sensitively. 'What you are doing is fine but you might like to consider an alternative way that works just as well, it not better'.

13 Whatever the level at which individual students are working, you should confirm their progress and their current levels of understanding and skill. People want to know how they are doing and positive reinforcement is both appreciated and motivating when it is offered in an adult and realistic manner.

14 Students are oblivious of you until they hit a snag or want some advice as to what to do next, *then* they want you, and they'd like you *now!* However, adults are reasonable and are willing to wait a while once they know you have noticed them. If you are busy with one individual then let them know they are next: '... after Josie, OK? I promised to help her next'. Adults don't demand equal amounts of your time – they recognise that some students have more need of help than others – but they do want fairness. They quite rightly want some part of your attention and to know that you are interested in their progress and success. Make sure that you visit everyone at least once a half-session and do not allow any one person to monopolise your time. Working 1:1 is tiring, give yourself time to catch your breath every now and again.

One danger of working with individual students is that you forget the rest of the class. Be conscious of what is happening behind and around you; check the group regularly and see if anyone needs you, is having trouble (or causing trouble) or has stopped working all together.

15 One of the benefits of 1:1 is that students are able to work at their own pace and not be held up or overtaken by others in the group. However, this freedom brings with it several riders.

– Some students come to resent any time spent in whole group teaching. Whilst it would be silly to do more than is necessary, there will be times that teaching the group or a sub group of students together is the most efficient and effective way of moving people on or helping them with an issue that they are all about to meet. It will also maintain a sense of group identity. You could begin each session with a short presentation period, and/or include a 10 minute slot at some stage during the session when you introduce something new, or invite students to describe something they are attempting, or raise a problem, or show them an item of interest.

– You need to monitor and keep some record of each student's development and progress. How you do this is up to you though some sort of spread sheet where you can make comments and/or tick off items each person has completed works well. Avoid holding it all in your head – it is good professional practice to maintain individual student records for your own reference, for quality assurance purposes, and for any substitute tutor who may have to take over the class. The act of recording student progress also means that you *have* to review and assess the work of each student, which in turn leads you to decide what help they may need from you and what they should do next.

– People working on their own make significant demands upon teaching and learning materials. The able student will get through more activities and exercises than another; the slower student needs to work on the critical ones and these may have to be simplified and/or extended. Select an adequate package of materials for a session or group of sessions that will satisfy the range of ability and skill in a logical, progressive sequence. Ensure that the additional items you include for the advanced students are worthwhile and make demands upon them, but also that everyone has tackled the basic items that ensure fundamental proficiency in the topic.

– There is no reason why people shouldn't seek help from each other – indeed cooperative learning is to be encouraged. However, watch out for the student who always seems to be asking a neighbour; the former needs your help and the latter needs some protection to allow him/her to get on with his/her own work. Watch out, too, for the class expert who may be functioning as a private tutor, and dispensing unhelpful and unasked for advice to others.

LECTURE/TALK (presentational; cognitive; plenary)

A formal lecture/talk – *a tutor discourse/presentation to a group of any size plus the major variant of presentation with group participation including a mixed economy of talk and activities* – provides information and ideas, usually within a specific period of time. Organised and structured knowledge can be offered with a sense of immediacy, enthusiasm, and excitement. A talk can develop an argument, outline or summarise a field of knowledge, pose questions and highlight issues.

1   A major problem in giving a lecture/talk is deciding how much to tell people. Most of us say much too much. Rethink your topic from the students' points of view and say only what they actually 'need to know' rather than what would be 'nice to know'. Being clear about the purpose and learning outcomes will also be of considerable help to you in selecting the optimum content.

2   A formal lecture/talk can be structured as a classical survey: 'there is X, there is Y and there is Z'; as a sequential description: 'there is X, which leads to Y, and therefore affects Z'; or via a problem centred approach: 'one possibility is x^1, y^1 and z^1, another is x^2, y^2, z^2'.

Each should use the same technique: an *orientation*, some *key points* and a *summary*. The opening or orientation should gain and hold attention. You need to motivate listeners as well as inform them, so devise a lead-in which will capture their interest. Instead of a bald statement of the topic, you could start with a reference to or a request for listeners' experience, an actual or rhetorical question, a relevant anecdote, a novel object, item, or picture, or an even a personal reference.

Explain each of your key points in turn, avoiding unnecessary technical terms and over-complex sentences. Use verbal markers to help people follow what you are saying:

– *signposts* indicate structure and direction: 'First, I want to outline what dietary fibre is; second where it occurs in our foodstuffs; third, to examine the ways in which it is of benefit to us ...'
– *frames* indicate the beginning and end of a subtopic: 'So those are the main characters. Let's now look at how they first meet ...'
– *foci* highlight and emphasize the key points: 'So the main points are to measure accurately and record your readings carefully'

   – *links* join one part of an explanation to another: 'You can now see that the French had a different concept of colonialism. This explains why they ...'

The summary is a restatement of the key points. Avoid introducing new ideas at this stage though you may use other words to rehearse what you have already said. The way that you link the key points together should lead to your conclusion, the answer to the question/problem posed at the outset. 'To sum up, let's look at the main points we've talked about.'

3 People's attention often wanders into 'micro-sleeps' after 20 minutes or so of sustained listening. You should therefore give them the opportunity to actively manipulate the ideas and information you are presenting – by allowing them to think about the point you have just made; recognise the example; extract the principle; examine the relationship between the new and what they already know. As a result they are much more likely to attend, learn and remember than if you allow them to sit passively, letting your words wash over them.

4 Use people's experience. Asking people to indicate their personal response by a show of hands is a minimal way. Asking for individual contributions, questions, answers and observations from the group involves them more actively, though to start with they may find it risky in front of others. (Tell them to work in pairs first and then ask for their joint view, thereby allowing them to share any feelings of exposure). Encourage people to draw their own conclusions. Let them come up with some of the principles involved rather than your telling them. Pose a question and give them time to think. Encourage them to try out their ideas on a partner, and then ask them if anyone would like to offer you a solution. People find it difficult to concentrate for long periods, so at least give them a brief break to stretch and to change their sitting positions every half an hour or so. Better still, use some of the activities we suggest here.

5   Relate your material to what listeners already know. Use examples and illustrations that are lucid, unambiguous and recognisable. Where the topic is new, draw analogies and examples to form bridges between what they already know and what they don't. Use examples that relate to their existing experience and think these out beforehand: don't hope that they will occur to you on the spur of the moment.

6   Write out what notes you feel you need, adding a simple time plan, the examples you want to offer, the resources and A/V aids you are going to use. Think about creating two sets: one of your content, the other your session plan. Underline or highlight the important points. Number the sheets (or record cards) and/ or attach them together. You will probably find that you need make only occasional reference to your notes anyway, since you have prepared them carefully beforehand. An OHP transparency(s) of the main points may provide you with all the prompts you require. Avoid reading out a written talk: it is always obvious and rarely done well. If you feel you really have to do so, write it as a radio script to be listened to, not as a journal article to be read.

7   Check your listeners' comprehension by looking for clues and cues of their interest, involvement and understanding. Ask obliquely if they understand: 'Are you happy so far or should I go over the main points ... I know that one or two are a bit difficult? People often take it as their fault (rather than your misjudgment!) that they haven't grasped something and they're usually reluctant to admit to it.

8   Audio/visual aids will nearly always add to what you are doing. Ask yourself: 'Why specifically don't I want to use them?' rather than 'Should I?' Make full use of resources and AVAs to illustrate and enhance what you have to say.

9   Effective presentation is about open communication. Read the chapter on self-presentation [27] which sets out some suggestions about verbal, extra verbal and non-verbal messages. Of all things,

be quietly enthusiastic and involve the group, respecting and acknowledging their adulthood.

10 The traditional question time at the end of a talk is often stilted and unsatisfactory, though it can work with a sophisticated audience. One solution is to finish in plenty of time and suggest to people they first discuss any questions they may have with the person sitting next to them. This way, a question can be legitimized as a worthwhile one to pose, and can be asked as 'We would like to know …' thus sharing the feeling of risk. Our approach is to encourage people to ask questions during the session. Why make them wait? If you know what is in their heads you can better modify and adapt what you are to do and say next to aid their understanding. If it happens that you are due to cover what is asked later on, then courteously say so.

LECTURE/TALK WITH GROUP PARTICIPATION
(presentational and interactive; cognitive; plenary)

The suggestions given above for a lecture/talk refer to tutor presentation where the level of active group participation is minimal. Listeners' physical passivity *might* be appropriate because of constraints of time, particular demands of the content, or where a period of quiet listening and reflection is called for. However, it is our opinion that this is not very often the case in ACL; indeed, you should be concerned if you find you are using non-participative talks at all frequently with any group of adults. Giving people a range of opportunities for active involvement with the material, the tutor, and with each other significantly enhances their knowledge, understanding, interest, motivation and subsequent transfer of learning.

1 Capitalise on people's existing knowledge, experience and abilities to provide examples, make judgments and draw conclusions. *Someone* will know *something* about whatever you have to say … and many a fair amount! It is much better that you discover earlier rather than later where such expertise and

experience lies. You can use what is known for the benefit of others (and it will spare you embarrassment when it is eventually revealed). Ask questions of the group during your talk ... and build on their answers. Fight shy of choosing a named individual unless s/he clearly wants to answer. Invite/welcome questions *from* the group during your presentation, too. Why keep them waiting until the end when their specific interest in it will have waned or their unsolved problem has resulted in further confusion?

2 Ask people to work informally with their neighbours as a buzz group to identify something, compare ideas, explain a connection, etc. Form small groups of 2, 3, 4 or 5 to work on a task, solve a problem, analyse an extract, interpret a map, etc. (Incidentally, using curved rows with a centre aisle allows for much better communication, interaction and ease of movement than does a cinema style layout, so rotate the room seating lengthways by 90° if you need to.)

3 Prepare handout copies of text extracts, diagrams, maps, pictures, photos, newspaper articles, etc, for whole group activities or small group work. Let people retain them to create their own reference resource.

4 Plan a sequence of activities to 'break up' your presentation. Use a range of procedures that will cause them to observe, identify, analyse, relate, compare, contrast, solve problems, etc, rather than simply listening to you doing it for them. You can confirm/correct/build upon their contributions thereafter. The variations are endless but some possibilities include:

A	B	C
Tutor talk	Group activity	Introduction
Buzz group	Brain storm	Video
Tutor talk	Tutor talk	Review of video
Slides	Individual task	Tutor talk
Questions	Pair work	Small groups
Tutor talk	Snowball	Plenary feedback
Tutor talk		

In each instance the tutor's presentation holds the subsidiary activities together, each of which can be easily organised even in a formal lecture theatre where the audience has to remain relatively static.

5   A number of subjects call for the use of slide photographs (35mm or PC projected images). There is an unfortunate tendency amongst some tutors to use a 'more the better' approach with a result that sessions become a voice-over slide show with little or no active participation. If you use slides, *severely* limit the number you show and actively involve people in the interpretation, discussion and application of what they are looking at. To this end, ask people to:

   –   identify the item, its family, its style, its location, a similar one, a contemporary one
   –   compare/contrast this one with the preceding one
   –   describe why/how it looks unusual, similar, different
   –   interpret its meaning, its symbolism, its size
   –   distinguish unusual features, colours, shapes
   –   ask questions of you – and each other – about it
   –   review a previous slide in the light of new ideas discussed.

6   The lecture/talk with group participation allows listeners to contribute and participate more, to experience a greater variety of opinion and information, and to interact with others and clarify their ideas. However you choose to structure your presentation, remember that adults respond to speakers who are warm, enthusiastic and stimulating. So smile and make it plain that you enjoy your subject, the opportunity of sharing it with others, and working with the group in front of you.

PROJECTS AND ASSIGNMENTS (interactive and self-enquiry; cognitive and affective; small group and individual)

Projects and assignments – *individual or group work undertakings* – allow people to reflect upon and make practical use of the ideas/

material addressed during the course. If a project is collaborative, it gives them the opportunity to cooperate, share, delegate and take on responsibilities for others. They also provide material for formal/ informal assessment of learning and progress.

1   Once the purpose and learning outcomes of individual projects and assignments have been identified, the content may either be specified or left to the student. You will have to decide how directive you need to be, depending upon how important it really is that a particular item is addressed in a particular way versus the desirability of learner independence. The less experienced may need rather more guidance. They may feel at a loss if they have no direction as to the identity of the topic, how something might be tackled, what could be included and how it can be set out. At the same time, people are likely to be more motivated and committed where they perceive the work is their own, so let them make choices where they can: eg the topic, the ways in which they work, and how to present the finished product.

2   As far as you can, provide the general resources needed to complete an assignment or project. Construct a list showing the cost and availability of specialist materials where they are called for. Encourage people to be adventurous and to make use of a range of additional materials and formats – pictures, tapes, articles, role play, etc. Confirm any assessment criteria to be used and agree the time scale. Provide ongoing constructive, formative feedback. Peer judgment made in concert with yours can prove of value since people will learn from judging the work of others as well as reflecting upon the group's observations of their individual pieces of work.

3   When you set up *group* projects and assignments, ensure that small groups do not spend too long deciding on why, what and how long, instead of getting on with it. Suggest that they may benefit from delegating tasks and/or designating a coordinator. If it is an extended project, build in session time for groups to meet and coordinate their work when you can also monitor their progress and offer guidance and support. If a project is to be

assessed, decide with them how contributing individuals are to be allocated grades.

QUESTIONS; SOCRATIC QUESTIONING (interactive; all domains; all groups)

Questions – *verbal interrogations intended to elicit recall, observation and/or thought* – involve individuals directly with material and can assess levels of knowledge, understanding, application and transfer.

1   Asking questions can be an integral part of most other methods and a method in itself – Socratic questioning. Questioning can serve a number of functions in addition to the checking and assessing of knowledge. It can stimulate interest, curiosity and motivation, elicit a person's knowledge for the benefit of others, focus and develop self-expression and logical/critical thought.

2   Ask questions one at a time, making them clear and straightforward, using words and concepts with which the group is familiar. Avoid those that require a preamble or explanation. Select the right focus and level. Open questions require broad and extended answers and they are likely to promote further discussion. Closed questions call for narrowly focused answers and are useful for drawing out specific facts and promoting deductive and inductive thought if you leave time for people to draw implications. (Watch out for 'Battleship' questions where you know the answer and they can only guess at what's in your head!)

3   Expect to direct questions at the group as a whole, rather than putting named individuals on the spot. Phrase a question so that everyone has a chance to respond. (There may be circumstances where you do wish to ask a question of a specific individual, but be sure *why* you want to.) Ask those who look ready to answer, and not only those who always appear to know. Give people time and use non-verbal signals such as eye contact and head nodding to encourage them.

4 Be positive and confirming when people answer correctly: 'That's right ... yes, good ... that's very perceptive', etc. Where people seem to be struggling, rephrase the question or suggest likely areas of response. If you don't understand an answer, ask the person to rephrase/explain it. Whilst you shouldn't accept a wrong answer, take care not to put the person down. 'Well, I'm not sure that is the case' is better than 'No!' Ensure the individual is not left feeling a public failure; find an opportunity to value him/her for a later, correct response or other positive act.

5 Refer back to individual answers made earlier in the session – 'As Mary said ... as Parveen told us'. This will further value participants' contributions, increase their self-confidence, and make them more willing to participate again. (It may be possible to make use of a previously wrong answer where some element of it fits into what you are currently considering.) Use people's answers to construct a framework of ideas and understanding, and make a note of the important responses on a flip chart.

6 Socratic Questioning uses a series of sequential questions, such that the answers lead cumulatively to an understanding of an issue or the solving of a problem. If you use this procedure, think out the major questions beforehand so that you are clear of the direction they will take the group.

7 The initial question(s) should be answerable from participants' existing knowledge with a succeeding question making use of the understanding and knowledge gained from a preceding answer. You will need to be flexible and to listen carefully so that you can adapt what you ask next to take account of answers already given. It is unlikely that you will want to base a whole session on Socratic questioning, but used appropriately, it provides variety and direction, and it has the particular benefit of involving people consciously in their own thinking processes.

8 As an example, a sequence of Socratic questions used with a photograph of a bus queue in a social psychology group might go as follows:

'We can see that these people are waiting for a bus behind the sign but why do you think that they are they standing apart from each other? ... Do the distances look about the same or are they very different? ... Is such standing at a distance just sheer chance or do people intend it? ... Are we conscious of doing it? ... How could we describe this tendency? ... In what other social circumstances is this comfort zone or 'personal space' apparent? ... When might people be willing to stand closer, or want to stand further away? ... Are people reluctant to being asked to 'close up'? ... How might you see them physically responding if they were? ... Where might the photograph have been taken? ... Would the pattern be different in another region/country? ... What if two of them were friends, then what? ... Why?'

RAINBOWING (interactive; cognitive and affective; small group)

Rainbowing – *a small group organisation involving discussion and reporting* – considerably increases participation and shares the product of small group work with other participants.

1 Rainbowing redistribute people into new groups such that a second group has a member each from a previous grouping. If the initial small groups are A, B and C, when reformed into new groups, new group 1 will have one member from group A, one from B, one from C; new group 2 will have (another) person each from groups A, B and C and so on. Rainbowing is most easily achieved where the total is divisible into three small groups of three, 4 groups of 4, 5 of 5, etc. Where this is not the case and you have students left over, ask them to work as conjoined twins. (With 10 people, the regrouping would be A+B+C; A+B+C; A+A+B+C.) If you are a person short, ask an individual to report briefly to one group and then join a second group and stay there. (With 15, you would end up with three new groups, each of A+B+C+D, and one of B+C+D only.)

2 Rainbowing allows for several permutations. You can ask the initial groups to discuss a topic, work on a problem, or identify

a plan of action. Then when they rainbow into new groups they report their original group's findings, compare it with those of their new partners and build on it. Other strategies include the initial groups working on different aspects of a problem, with the second, reformed groups, coordinating the separate parts into a whole. Alternatively, the first groups go so far with a task, then complete it in their new groupings.

3   Everyone *must* participate as they need to understand and record what their first group decides and then report it to their new group. They are more likely to be involved in the discussion as they have to own what they report. It also means that each individual works directly with a larger number of other group members than would otherwise happen.

4   You will need to explain the procedure with care so that people understand exactly what they are to do. Monitor and coordinate what takes place within groups and initiate the changeover at the point when the second groupings can begin at the correct stage.

ROLE PLAY (interactive; all domains; small group)

Role Play –*the spontaneous acting out of a character/role within a situation* – provides a 'real life' experience and new insights into the feelings, thoughts and actions of the characters involved. It facilitates understanding and transfer through experience and empathy.

1   Role play provides experience of the realities and perceptions of others. However, there may be people in the group who have had poor previous experiences of the method and you should introduce it carefully. Helpful synonyms include: 'Seeing how it feels to be X or Y', and 'Trying out how the situation feels before we talk about ...' They should know at the start that they are free to participate or not, especially if there are emotional areas involved. Establish mutual trust and confidentiality, and agree that no one should be made fun of.

2   Do not begin to set up a role play until the previous activity is at rest and everyone is ready. Make it abundantly clear why you are asking people to participate and what you hope they will get out of it. Describe what you want them to do, with whom, for how long and whether there will be any observers. You may need an outline plot or statement of the situation, though not a script. Say how you propose they should share their experiences afterwards. Once the activity is fully understood, set up the small groups required, confirm that people know who is to go first, then monitor what transpires, intervening sensitively if necessary.

3   Once the action is complete, give plenty of time for people to debrief out of their role(s) by talking through aspects of each other's actions and statements. Only then seek feedback about the role feelings engendered, lessons learnt and new perceptions gained. You can ask small groups to work together, or take reports from observers if you have used them.

4   Ensure that you help people make good use of their newly-gained experience. Follow any role play by considering the implications for present understanding and future action: 'so if that is what it feels like, what does it mean for us/you? How can we use what we now know to change or modify *X* or *Y*?'

SEMINAR/STUDENT PRESENTATION (interactive; cognitive and affective; small group)

A seminar – *a smaller group meeting, usually with one or more students offering a prepared piece to the others* – stimulates individuals to research a subject and gives the opportunity for participants to present their findings and/or lead a discussion.

1   Though seminars *per se* are more common in higher education they also work well with adult students, though they're usually known as short student presentations and even 'show and tell'. What ever the exact format, the opportunity to carry out

research, prepare and present material, answer questions, lead a discussion, etc, can prove of significant benefit to those undertaking it.

2   You should agree the contributors, topics and timings well in advance. (Some people may be horrified by the prospect and be unwilling to undertake even an informal procedure, so make it voluntary unless there are imperative reasons why they *should* do it.) Allow people to negotiate with you and between themselves as to who is to do what and when, the format, resources, and so on. If there is benefit in the group carrying out some preparatory reading/activity so that they are more receptive to what is to be offered, agree it with them.

3   Support and advise individuals in their preparation and planning. It will be helpful if you provide a general guide of how to do things, offer help about what they might read and/or provide a source list to help them get started. Make time for them to consult with you as they have need. If you have doubts about someone's content and/or their approach, you could change the order to allow more time, offer to work with them in support, or do a 'double act' with them.

4   Expect to informally chair the session, and to help out if you're needed: it isn't a *viva voce* examination. Make sure that no one switches off, especially those who have already done their presentations. Thank the individual publicly (and privately afterwards) and offer positive and constructive feedback. Carry the topic forward and relate what has just been learnt both to what has already been covered and to what is to come.

SIMULATION (interactive; all domains; small group)

Simulation – *a structured, lifelike situation* – gives access to real happenings in a safe, controlled situation, with the opportunity for analysing, modifying and replaying the action a second or third time. It facilitates decision-making, management and transfer.

1   When you set up a simulation, you should try to create as lifelike a situation as possible: specify roles, background details and materials for each participant. You may want to write an outline script. Consider providing items of dress as they can promote involvement and commitment to the characters. Hats work well. If the simulation is skills practice, use an appropriate range of props, equipment and resources.

2   Follow the same procedures as for role play in setting the learning outcomes, briefing participants, allowing any individual to opt-out, managing the timing and action, and providing sufficient debriefing opportunities before you take in any feedback. You may need extra time for people to acquaint themselves with the details of their roles and to set up a sequence of events. Consider whether this could be done in the preceding session, giving participants time to grow into and elaborate their characters.

3   A variation, 'In basket', involves modification of the ongoing action. New information is fed into the plot, additional resources are offered, or something is deemed to have broken down to see how people can cope and modify their plans.

4   Like role play, it is crucial that you follow the feedback session with a consideration of the implications of what has been learnt and experienced. You cannot assume that people either can or will undertake this transposition once the action has finished. Indeed, some of the reluctance of people to undertake further role play and simulation exercises springs from a lack of purposeful outcome of these experiential methods. 'Knowing how it feels' and 'what it is like' are not of themselves adequate preparation for future action. Plan time for the group to discuss what they have understood from their experiences, to draw up some best practice guidelines and/or to prepare an action schedule.

SNOWBALLING (interactive; cognitive and affective; plenary)

Snowballing – *a group organisation involving evaluation and negotiation* – distills people's ideas by negotiation. It requires participants to evaluate alternative propositions and increases participation.

1 Snowballing involves the progressive distillation of ideas, proposals or answers as the numbers of participants increase. This inversion is achieved by asking people to negotiate the importance of their ideas with others in such a way that the each new partnership agrees on the most critical items from their several proposals. People have to be willing to argue and compromise though it does need to be fun ... and usually is.

2 Ask people to work on their own to produce W number of points, before sharing these with a partner. These two then work together to agree on the most important of their joint list ($W+W$) to arrive at X points – which *must* be less that W. Ask each pair to join another pair, whereupon each quartet, with two list X items long, compare and negotiate an agreed list Y items long – which *must* in its turn be less than X. If the group is large enough, quartets can be combined together to form octets to produce a new list of Z items. The plenary group can then vote and/or prioritise the *2, 3 or 4 Z* lists produced by the octets.

3 You will need to think through the numbers you need. Were you to have 24 in a plenary group, your task would be easy. If you want to end up with 6 items in total from the whole group, plan for 5 items from individuals, 4 items from each pair, 3 items from each quartets, and 2 items from the 3 octets. Where the numbers of participant are less easily subdivided, you will need some people to work on their own and others working as conjoined twins though these latter may only produce the same number of items as they would have done had they worked as individuals.

4 Snowballing demands tight management and control as it generates a lot of noise and excitement. Explain how it works and be sure that everyone knows what they are being asked to

do. It will prove less confusing if you say which group is to join up with which *at the point you want it done* rather than expecting people to remember all the moves from the start. Give out the problem/question only when you are sure they understand that they must arrive at the exact number of items you specify each time and how it's all going to work out.

TUTORIAL; PRIVATE INTERVIEW (interactive; cognitive and affective; individual)

A tutorial – *an arranged, private discussion between student and tutor* – provides a safe environment to follow up issues and areas of interest, to offer consultation and supervision, to carry out/agree some assessment, and to give personal support and confirmation.

1   Tutorials are less usual in ACL than in higher education though the learning opportunities that these one-to-one meetings have are considerable. The initiative should stay as much with the student as with the tutor, so that the former can follow up his/her own needs, ideas and feelings.

2   Agree the purpose, areas of interest, confidentiality and timing with the group beforehand if one-to-one meetings are to be available to all. People should know what is involved, what they need to prepare and how long they will each get with you. Provide as private, comfortable and secure setting for the discussion as you can. Avoid obvious barriers of desks, harsh back lighting or eyeball-to-eyeball seating arrangements. Sit obliquely to each other. Confirm what is to be covered by asking the student to outline his/her agenda first. Where you judge that it is inappropriate for you to address a particular issue say so and give your reasons. Agree any additional items that you think should be discussed. The dialogue that takes place should be between adults meeting as equals, so take time and care to establish the right atmosphere for this to happen. Note down the key points of your discussion for later reference.

3   Work through the agenda without haste, giving time and space for the more difficult issues. Listen more and talk less. Offer appropriate yardsticks for the individual's progress, confirming and supporting him/her as necessary. Where you need to confront someone with some aspect of his/her behaviour, do it in a manner that allows him/her to retain their self-respect. Help the student to identify ways in which a difficulty may be resolved rather than you prescribe it for him/her. Negotiate and agree any action plans that s/he – or you – is to undertake. Finish the discussion on a positive note and thank the individual for his/her time.

VISIT; FIELD TRIP (interactive; cognitive and psycho-motor; plenary)

Visits and field trips – *direct access to the real world of the topic* – allow people to find out information first hand, handle artifacts, observe a process or put theory/skills into practice.

1   Undertake a preliminary visit and make contact with any site personnel involved. Ensure that the particular elements with which you want the group to engage will be available. Establish the availability of car parking, lavatories, refreshments, and access for participants with disabilities. Undertake a risk assessment. Collect any literature, including location maps and directions. (If students are to organise the trip on behalf of the group, agree that they keep you fully briefed and that you retain the final say about last minute amendments. The overall responsibility remains yours if the trip is an official part of the course.)

2   Sometime before the event, discuss the purpose/learning outcomes of the visit with the group and outline what will be required in terms of activity, cost, dress, etc, and that everyone who wants to attend can do so. (The new Disabled Discrimination Act (DDA) legislation can mean you would have to cancel a visit if the special needs of all students cannot be met.) Confirm legal and insurance responsibilities, describe any risks and agree health/safety matters. Collect 'phone numbers for a telephone tree and agree a contingency plan for late arrivals, weather, etc.

3   Most visits are likely to be an integral part of the course, so prepare and brief people beforehand about what they should look out for. Find out how the group would like to undertake the on-site visit and/or be guided and negotiate some best practice. If you are using local guides, find out their normal practices and the extent to which they can adapt to the wishes/needs of the group. Avoid 'myopia by handout' (where people spend so much time with printed material they fail to see what is around them) and 'talking to a standstill' (where you or a guide describes too much for too long) Any on site teaching must allow for distractions, brain fag and physical fatigue. Ensure that people have sufficient time to observe on their own, and that you have planned that the necessary personal facilities will be to hand at the appropriate times.

4   Schedule session time after the visit to consider what people understood about what they saw, heard and did … and what they learnt!

KEY POINTS

- *Choose methods that will provide variety and interest as well as helping students achieve particular knowledge and skills efficiently and effectively*
- *Give time and thought to the management of a chosen method so that you are on top of the 'when', 'where' and 'how' of its use.*

17 Working with Small Groups

The chapters on managing methods [16] and devising activities [20] provide details of managing particular small group methods and of selecting appropriate tasks. This chapter identifies some practical issues about arranging and monitoring small group work, and how to manage feedback.

1 Whilst there are no hard and fast rules about the optimum size of small groups, what you choose will need to reflect what you want people to do, how much time you have available and how many people there are in total. As small group size increases from two to six, so the time needed to complete a task increases, though this is balanced by fewer groups needing to feed back. Whatever you settle on, you may still have to work out what to do with the 'left over' student.

2 The composition of small groups can be based upon:

   – a free-for-all
   – the register ... or *1,2,3; 1,2,3* ... or name badge colour or letter code
   – 'work with someone you know ... don't know ... haven't yet worked with'
   – similar or dissimilar background/experience
   – same or different gender
   – more advanced and less advanced students
   – mixed experience.

   The choice you make will be determined by the nature of a particular small group activity and the learning outcome(s) it is to serve.

3 Ensure that there is enough equipment and resources to go round, whether pencils or video cameras. People will want to get on and not be bothered with missing resources or requests

from other groups. Plan sufficient time to distribute what is needed and for people to familiarise themselves with any novel item before you start. If you are using different small group rooms, check beforehand that the furniture is set out and that the resources needed are in place.

4   Telling people just once what you want them to do is rarely sufficient, so first explain what the task is, then tell them how it is to be done ... and write it all on a handout or flipchart if it is at all complicated. Check that everyone has understood and that they know 'what, how, how long, with whom, and how they are to feedback their results'. You can expected that even when you've explained the activity and the group organization, *and* written it down, there will still be some who aren't quite sure, so ask if any clarification is required. As people organise themselves, be on hand to advise and facilitate their getting started. If you are using small group rooms, go round and check that they've started.

5   Decide how you are going to monitor each small group, especially if they are in different locations. Minimally you should walk round quietly every so often, listening unobtrusively, though in fact it is quite possible to watch and listen in to several groups working in the same room without moving. (You *can* sit in with a group, but be aware that you will alter the dynamic and they will defer to you. You need to have a good reason to join a group and generally speaking, it is better not to do so.) If you are happy with what people are doing, let them get on with it. Should you discover there is some general misunderstanding, make an announcement; if it is just one group, speak to them quietly. Avoid leaving the room as any protracted absence will be adversely noted; use the time to prepare for the next section. Warn everyone that there is about 'X minutes left. Should people need a lot more time, or if they are working quicker than you expected, modify the timing. Assess when most groups have come to an appropriate end point then jolly up the last ones. Avoid having everyone waiting for the slow group, however assiduously they may be working.

6 You must value at least some of the work of every group. People want to tell you – and the others – what they have achieved. However, avoid asking every group to share everything as it becomes tedious. (Where you feel you *have* to this, choose a group to go first that you thing will be brief and to the point. They will provide the model for the rest.) You might use one of the following feedback procedures:

   – Request each group to select and prioritise two or three points. Then ask the first group for one of their points, the next group for one of theirs, and so on. This way everyone will make a contribution, offering a second and third choice if their first has already been given.
   – Choose one group and ask them to report back with other groups, adding any important items or ideas that *they* have identified that the reporting group missed out. (Chose another group next time.)
   – Give each group a sheet of flipchart paper (or an OHP acetate) and ask them to write up 'X' of their items. Show an example sheet so that they can see that you want 'N lines ... this big ... set out in this way'. Put them up on the wall with *Blu-Tack*®; double them over so that you can reveal all of them at once. Ask the whole group to read each sheet and note the similarities/differences.
   – Give each group one/two/three strips of card to write down their best point(s) then display them using a drawing pin, *Blu-Tack*® or a *Velcro*® board. You can rearrange them into categories at will.

7 A major problem of receiving oral feedback from a number of groups is making sense of the suggestions as they come in and ordering them in ways that you can use afterwards. One efficient procedure is to identify the likely responses beforehand and prepare areas on the board or flip chart in which to write them. You can then put each idea down in an appropriate category as it is offered. If you edit what is said, check that they are happy with your new wording.

8   Methods that involve personal identification and/or emotional responses such as role play, simulation and other experiential procedures call for careful handling. Before you collect in the feedback, give people 'debriefing' time; let them unwind by telling their partners how the experience *actually* felt, especially if it caused any real emotional reaction towards the other person. When everyone feels comfortable, sample their responses using one of the ways suggested above. Once you have identified what has been learnt from the experience, build upon this awareness by discussion or a related activity: 'How should an interview be conducted to alleviate these problems ... what practical adaptations would improve someone's daily living ... how can we modify our use of language to obviate discrimination?'

KEY POINTS

- *Small group work needs careful planning and management.*
- *Recognise and value at least some of the results of each small group.*

18 Working with a Large Group

Working with large groups of 40–50+ calls for changes in emphasis and modification of approach rather than a new set of skills, since the same principles of adult learning and teaching apply. Most of the strategies and techniques which are successful with smaller groups can work as well with larger ones, though careful planning and confident management are needed. Understandably, the size of the group and of the room can seem daunting at first, but once initial nervousness has dissipated, sessions with a large group can be exhilarating.

1   Working with a large group does not mean that you have to use presentational methods; there are other and often better ways of working than giving formal talks. Nevertheless, you *may* need to do so, because of the particular purpose of the session and/or its learning outcomes. For these reasons – and not because giving a talk is the optimum method – we begin with it here.

   –   Structuring a lecture or talk, and the important aspects of explaining, are described in the managing methods chapter [15], but one or two points are worth restating. Choose a lecture type (problem-solving, classical or sequential) to suit the content and the learning outcomes. Use the sequence: orientation > key points > summary. For once, an old chestnut is appropriate: 'Say what you are going to say, say it and say that you've said it'. Use a range of organisers (signposts, frames, foci, links, and key points) and tell the group what you hope to cover and how you propose to structure the material – *X* sections and *Y* points.

   –   Employ a range of varied but recognisable examples and analogies. Say the same thing in a different way if an idea is at all difficult since this gives a further opportunity for people to think about it and to see it in relation to what they already know.

- Write out what notes you feel you need, with a simple time plan, the examples you want to give, the A/V aids you are going to use, etc. Underline or highlight the important points. Number the sheets or record cards and/or attach them together. You will probably find that you need make only occasional reference to your notes anyway. Avoid reading a prepared text not only because it always sounds obvious, but it also makes it difficult for you to interact with the group, make eye contact, take questions or make much use of their contributions. If you *have* to, write it as a radio script. Think Alistaire Cooke.

2 In addition to the standard range of resources and AVAs, most of which lend themselves to work with large groups, you might also consider:

- bringing in someone else to do a short celebrity spot on his/her speciality. Be sure s/he's fully briefed on what you want done
- use an actor or someone else to simulate a role or injury. (Use great circumspection with a real patient or client: everyone, including the group, must give their consent.)
- act out a piece of role-play with a prepared stooge
- show a 'piece to camera' of you video recorded in an appropriate setting.

3 The benefits of active student participation cannot be overstressed. Consequently, when you are working with a large group, think about ways that you can structure a session to maximise their interaction with the material, with you and with each other. We have already suggested the following possibilities:

A	B	C
Tutor talk	Group activity	Introduction
Buzz group	Brain storm	Video
Tutor talk	Tutor talk	Review of video
Slides	Individual task	Tutor talk
Questions	Pair work	Small groups
Tutor talk	Snowball	Plenary feedback
	Tutor talk	

and there are other potential ways of arranging things, if you make use of the whole range of methods and resources. They will all work if you prepare well and manage things with confidence and enthusiasm. You could also:

- ask for 'hands-up' to indicate 'Who does what? Who agrees/ disagrees? Who has most/least?' etc.
- invite people to call out their responses/observations/ questions to slides, objects, verbal propositions, etc. It is easy enough to pick out two or three even from a cacophony of responses and to use a right one (or a wrong one) to carry things forward
- use buzz groups. Monitor what people say to each other and use the results in what you do next. These quick, informal dialogues function as mini breaks and give you an opportunity to reorganise
- use brainstorming. Ask for single words and record a sample of responses rather than all of them. It can be fun, especially if you ham it up a bit, though you must still value what is offered
- organise group work (as groups of 2, 3 or 4). Ask people to work with the person in the next seat and/or turn round to those behind. Check to see that every one has a partner(s) and bring together those who haven't. Ensure the task is clear to everyone. Use a handout or an OHP in addition to explaining verbally what you want them to do
- devise a variety of different tasks and activities such as: solve a problem, read an extract or précis, agree a response/answer with a partner(s), study and respond to photographs/ diagrams, debate an issue with a partner taking sides, role-play a situation, practice a technique, teach each other. Some activities can include an observer who offers feedback to his/ her partners (and to you). Repeat any role-based activity so that everyone plays each part in turn
- snowball and rainbow [16]
- ask the whole group to simulate a phenomenon or piece of behaviour eg a wave motion, a DNA molecule, discords and harmonies, speech rhythms or Greek chorus.

4   It has been pointed out several times that participatory activities must be monitored, shared and valued. Such feedback should be used with a large group too, though it needs to be carefully managed and is likely to be more perfunctory. You will not be able to hear from every small group – and people will recognise this – but you can sample what a few have done. Get the flavour by asking two or three pairs/trios to call out one of their more important ideas and then seek the whole group's confirmation that these represent the general opinion. Ask whether what you overheard – X, Y and Z – as you monitored some of the discussions are, in fact, what most people identified. The management of such plenary feedback calls for a degree of fairground theatricality. Make it fun and keep it moving even though it has the important purpose of demonstrating and reinforcing what they've learnt.

5   Negotiate with the group about their preference for asking questions either during or after the session. End-of-session question time often results in silence, so if this *is* what is agreed, give people time to check out a potential question(s) with a partner to confirm that it is worth asking. It allows pairs to ask the question: 'We would like to know …' thus sharing the risk of exposure. They could also write questions on cards, which you collect and shuffle, answering as many as you have time for.

   Our strong preference is for questions 'during' rather than 'after'. They indicate levels of people's interest, the ongoing links they're making with other ideas, and their overall understanding and learning. Such feedback allows a tutor to amend what is to come in the light of what has apparently been assimilated, and to emphasise what seems to be of interest, relevance or difficulty. Most importantly, it changes the flow of communication and involves people more directly.

6   Assessing the extent to which individuals are learning during a session (and what they have learnt by the end) isn't easy with any group, especially a large one. Evaluating how they are reacting to the session and what they thought about it at the end is less problematic. Where you subsequently meet individuals

and small groups in tutorials and workshops, or where they carry out some formal assessment procedure, you will be able to follow up the learning outcomes. But in addition, you could:

– watch for cues and clues. Identify whether people are attentive, enthusiastic, and alert to nuances, responsive to requests and/or taking notes; chatting, yawning or even asleep
– ask people to review what has been covered so far, say after 20 minutes, then write a brief collaborative résumé
– suggest they explain some/all of the main points to a partner and/or note down (with a partner's help) what else they need to do/read/practice to master a topic
– ask questions. They can be problem solving, factual, critical opinion, etc. Avoid directing questions at identified individuals, even though responses to generally addressed questions may be slow in coming. You could also ask people to work on an answer together, or to check each other's suggestion
– asking 'Do you understand?' usually elicits uncertain 'Yeses'. So ask obliquely: 'Are you happy … should I go over anything once again to be sure … can I pick up any points for clarification?'
– use test or quizzes that aren't too formal, serious or competitive; the main purpose for learners is to find out for themselves what they know … and collaborative work will tell you (and each individual) nearly as much. Ask them to label a diagram, draw a flow chart, re-order items, true/false, note down the X important features of Y, etc. Strike a balance between being too threatening and too simplistic.

7 Employ a short and simple evaluation which is completed on the spot, and returned. For all that tick box evaluations are quick, rough and ready, they are nearly always too quick, too rough and too ready. They won't tell you much. Asking for three or four short written responses is not overly burdensome – especially when you make it plain that you really do want their opinions. Let them collaborate. Why not? Include an item: 'What are you taking away with you of value?'

Organise the time so that the evaluation is completed at least 5 minutes before the end, allowing you to finish with a punchy finale. Be on hand as they leave to earwig comments. Ask people informally as they leave what use the session has been to them and what they've got out of it.

KEY POINTS

- *Use a range of strategies and techniques to provide both variety and interest.*
- *Look for ways in which people can actively participate more and you can talk less.*

---

19 Teaching and Learning Resources

Using teaching and learning resources, whether audio visual aids (AVAs), materials, objects or people, not only make the whole classroom process more interesting and enjoyable but also help tutors to teach more effectively and adult students to learn more efficiently. This is not to say that every session requires a pantechnicon of aids and resources, for in a few cases they can be a distraction, but generally speaking their use is beneficial.

1 The choices of what to use and when to use it depend upon:

  - the particular properties of a resource that will enhance learning
  - the likely response from the group
  - the cost-benefit outcome, ie increased student learning versus your tutor time, cost and effort in making/preparing the resource
  - your level of skill and experience in using it.

  Quality is important. Take time and trouble to produce/acquire/ use high standard resources. If it is apparent that you have made an effort, your students are likely to show interest and respond; give them stuff on the back of an envelope and that is what they will offer in return. When you create something of quality that works, store it for later use.

2 Be sure you know how to use the resource, especially the hardware. Work on the principle that if AVA technology can go wrong, it probably will! Find out how to operate *that* particular model in advance, and discover how to restore a connection, change a bulb, replace a fuse, etc. Identify the best working position in the room and the optimum seating plan for its use; check (again) that it is working before students arrive. Have a Plan B should a key AVA or resource suddenly become unavailable, such as a bulb and a replacement both blow, an internet connection cannot be made, or promised material is unavailable.

3   Observe the variety of objects and ideas that other tutors use. Keep a look out around the home and in toy and hobby shops for possible teaching aids; kitchen shops are a surprisingly good source. Steal ideas unashamedly and modify them for your own use. Be creative in the ways you use AVAs and resources. Enlist the help of your students. People have a houseful of objects and most will readily bring in some object they have and/or lend it to you. Others will have particular skills and be happy to construct something for your use with the group.

4   Some learning resources:

Audio/Visual Aids

Overhead projector	Digital projector	Interactive board
Laptop/PC	Video recorder	Video camera
Tape recorder	Television	Radio
Microscope	Slide projector	Flip chart
Writing boards	Display board	*Velcro*® board

Materials

Books	Handouts	Photocopies
Internet off prints	Original documents	Reports
Periodicals/Journals	Newspapers	Magazines
Comics	Photographs	Charts/posters
Tutor manuals	Student manuals	Catalogues
Promotional/publicity		

Objects

The real thing	Models	Samples
Specimens	Toys	Simulations

Outside events/visits:

Museums	Lectures	Field trips
Sports/leisure centres	Exhibitions	Conferences
Cinema/theatre/concert	Specialist outlet events	

5 All the following AVA tips and ideas that have been used successfully. If you can employ any of them, well and good, but use these as catalysts for your own ideas:

- give out old hats for role play characterisation
- use a teddy bear to represent an emotive figure – a deceased relative, an accident victim or an aggressive client
- replace the glass of a large picture frame with brushed nylon fabric; use *Velcro®* sticky pads to display a blown-up photograph of the individual/scene/item being discussed
- play music before/during a session: 'Pictures at an Exhibition' in a painting class; Prokofiev's 'Romeo & Juliet' in aggression studies; folk songs/Gregorian chant/Walton's 'Richard III' in a history group
- hang up an adapted nursery mobile to represent a process in equilibrium
- burn a marked candle in a water saucer to represent a time span
- use large *Post-it®* memos to collect and display the group's ideas
- put plain sticky labels over cheap playing cards and use them to distribute roles/activities/tasks/running order; students choose one from the fan you hold out
- take digital camera photos/35mm slides of any aspect of your subject and keep them for later use
- use a consistent type face and layout for all your handouts, and design a personal logo to identify them
- up end a largish table and rest its bottom edge on a chair; use it as an emergency flip chart stand. Take care!
- invite another tutor/practitioner/client/recipient/manufacturer to talk about 'the business' from his/her perspective
- keep some 6×4 inch blank record cards for a 'spontaneous' group activity: it looks more planned than asking students to 'find a bit of paper'
- repeatedly use a photocopier to enlarge diagrams
- have some simple sweets (Polo's, wine gums) to hand round
- though there are plenty of PC clip art sources, collect line drawings, cartoons, etc, from newspapers and magazines to illustrate OHPs and handouts.

6   Build up a book box library. Start with a few well-labelled books of your own and/or borrow others on long loan from the library. You *could* ask students to pay a small fee when they borrow something and use the cash to buy additional books for the box. People may also be willing to lend or even contribute a volume, though take care you don't end up as a repository for out-of-date texts! A simple loan sheet will suffice – who's borrowed what and when; the system is rarely abused.

7   Never go anywhere without your teaching/training box. Find a suitable container – from a large pencil case to a tool carry-all – for your equipment. Your subject will determine the specialist items you will need, but some general items that tutors keep by them include:

Ballpoint pens	Hole punch	Pencil sharpener
Blank sound tapes	Highlight pens	Pen knife
Blank videos	Kitchen 'pinger'	Phone card
Blu-Tack®	Masking tape	Receipt book
Bottle opener	Mints/fruit gums	Record cards
Calculator	Mobile phone	Rubber
Card (A4)	Nail file	Rubber bands
Chalk	Name badges	Ruler
Corkscrew	Needle & cotton	Safety pins
Craft knife	OHP acetates	Screwdriver
Dog clips	OHP pens (water	Scissors
Double adaptor	based)	*Sellotape*®
Drawing pins	OHP pens	Small change
Dressmaking pins	(permanent)	Spare bulbs
Elastoplast®	OHP pen eraser	Stapler
Envelopes	Paper (A4)	Staple remover
Extension lead	Paper clips	String
Flip chart paper	Pain-killers	*Tippex*®
Felt tip pens	Postage stamps	Tissues
Floppy discs	*Post-it*® (various)	Torch
Glue stick	Pencils	Travelling clock
		Whiteboard pens

8   Which ever projection AVAs you use, the same general points apply:

   – ensure that the screen is large enough. Consider projecting
     onto a pale coloured wall or build a screen with A1 paper
     and *Blu-Tack*®
   – ensure that everyone can see easily
   – instead of a too-high stand or table, place the projector on a
     reversed chair. Mark the position on the floor with chalk for
     easy repositioning
   – switch off when it's not needed
   – think about where to position yourself. Stand to the side of
     the screen by all means but stay out of the illumination
   – use a pointer or laser, not your finger + your arm, shoulder
     and head!
   – restrict the number of slides you show in any particular
     sequence; people get fatigued, especially if you aren't actively
     involving them.

• When you use an overhead projector (OHP):
   – avoid shape distortion of the projected image by keeping
     the screen and the upper OHP lens parallel
   – clean lenses and glass surfaces with a cloth
   – check that it is not too noisy. If it is, replace it
   – lay a ridged pencil on the acetate as a pointer.

• OHP acetates/transparencies are best made using a PC:
   – print a computer-designed item – your own or with
     PowerPoint® – directly onto a dry toner acetate sheet via
     a laser printer; use inkjet acetates if this is the type of
     printer you have
   – prepare a hard copy paper original and photocopy it onto
     a dry toner acetate sheet; check that it *is* the right acetate
     for a photocopier!
   – use at least 18 pt bold type face
   – limit the amount of data on a slide (7 lines @ 7 words
     each)
   – keep OHP acetates interleaved with paper; catalogue and
     store them in polythene folders held in a binder.

- OHP acetates can be hand lettered with non permanent/ water-soluble or with permanent/spirit-based OHP pens:

  - use only black and primary coloured, medium tipped pens
  - obtain an eraser fluid pen for use with permanent pens
  - place a sheet of lined paper underneath as a guide and leave 3+ cms at the top and bottom
  - A4 are best as square cardboard mounts are difficult to store
  - avoid using a continuous roll unless you have a good hand. If you do, use water soluble pens and write in randomised blocks not straight lines.

- Make OHP overlays by combining two or more acetates and hinging them with masking tape – not something like *Sellotape®* as it looks dirty when projected. You can also use OHP strips by cutting out 'bordered' items from a transparency and displaying them as you speak about each. Make an A4 transparency of a supermarket trolley or wire basket to use as a visual receptacle for a bunch of strips.

- A linked digital projector + lap top system allows any document, image or scanned-in item held on a computer to be displayed. The price of these projectors puts them beyond the means of most tutors though the nature of your subject might justify the expense. Teaching venues are becoming better equipped but you should not count on there being digital projectors *in situ* in every classroom (except in ICT suites) and there may well be high demand for portable ones. When you use one:

  - be sure that you are very familiar with the system's operation
  - boot up before the session starts and use a blank screen saver
  - avoid having the group watch a series of key stroke images whilst you get to the first image proper. It is *very* annoying.

- *PowerPoint®* presentations via a digital projector would appear to be the answer to everything. However, some groups groan audibly where they suspect 'death by multiple images'. So:

  - limit the numbers of slides you plan to show: everything you say does *not* need to be hammered home by yet another image
  - avoid making slides too fussy, too messy or over colourful. *PowerPoint®* doesn't take into account the principles of adult learning, perceptual overload, or taste
  - some tutors hide behind the *PowerPoint®* projection process and end up as push key/voice over automata
  - *PowerPoint®* presentations deter student participation, so you will need to work hard to encourage interaction
  - photocopied handouts of the slide summary printouts can be helpful but they are not the same as learning *per se*
  - Use *PowerPoint®* to enhance your teaching, not to replace you.

- Interactive boards (IBs) are the most recent electronic AVA addition, and are to be found in training suites and mainstream educational institutions. In essence, a digital projector shines a lap top screen's display onto an electronic screen (at least 1.5-metre square) which can then be touched with a pen so that the computer 'thinks' it is a mouse click. The unique features are that the tutor and students can interact with the computer from the front, and it is possible to 'write' using an electronic pen directly on the IB – and thus the PC – without using the keyboard. The system can also be used to show video/DVD/CD ROM material when linked to a sound system, and IB boards can be fixed or mobile. However 'all singing and dancing' this system seems – and it *can* practically do both – it is still an aid and not a tutor replacement. There is a danger that so much time and effort is put into designing the visual and auditory display that the purpose and learning outcomes of a session get lost.

- 35-mm slides (and digital camera images for digital projection) are easy to take and bring the outside into the classroom. Slide projectors are relatively robust and portable, and though bulbs do blow, their simple technology makes them easy to use and maintain.

- Severely limit the total number of slides you show. Avoid self indulgence; a couple of good images will be more effective than a dozen, however esoteric you believe them to be. When you use slides, work to involve people actively by inviting them to:

  - name the item, its family, its style, its location, a similar one, a contemporary one
  - compare/contrast this one with the preceding one
  - describe why/how it looks unusual, similar, different
  - interpret its meaning, its symbolism, its size
  - distinguish unusual features, colours, shapes
  - ask questions of you (and of each other)
  - review a previous slide in the light of new ideas discussed.

9   Writing/application surfaces

- Flip charts (FC)

  - use black + primary colour medium tipped FC pens
  - print, write large, and keep wordage to a minimum
  - stand away so people can see
  - fix A1 sheets on the wall with *Blu-Tack®* to give more writing space
  - use *appliqué* shapes, flash cards, symbols, etc, with *Blu-Tack®*
  - prepare sheets beforehand and keep them covered
  - use thicker paper and *Blu-Tack®* as a revealing technique
  - trace in 'spontaneous' items/lists/category slots in faint pencil beforehand
  - use jumbo paper clips to hold several sheets together, and coloured thumb tabs for easy location.

- Writing boards (white boards/chalk boards)

  - wipe the board clean before the session starts
  - write large in straight lines ... and without screeching
  - use only black + primary colour dry marker pens on a white board, and ensure you have an eraser and fluid
  - use only white/yellow chalk on a chalk board; have a duster to hand.

- Brushed nylon surface + *Velcro*®

  - use professional display materials or obtain some sticky-backed *Velcro*® and a board covered in appropriate fabric. This up-dated flannel graph is ideal for building up a chart, flow diagram, and so on, using prepared items
  - use large, colour-contrasted items, simple lettering and diagrams
  - quite heavy objects can be supported with *Velcro*® stickies
  - support the board on the ledge of a flip chart stand or set up linked boards as a free standing unit
  - buy a piece of brushed nylon fabric as an easy-to-carry and tack-up surface.

10   Video/DVD/tape recordings

- Playback

  - review all of a video/DVD/sound tape before using it
  - note the exact timings and be sure the new counter is zeroed
  - make your own DVD/tape of extracts using 2 recorders
  - go forwards only; if you plan to replay an earlier piece for comparison, record it a second time ie $A->B->C->B$.
  - introduce it, say why you're showing it to the group and tell them what to look out for. Follow it up afterwards
  - restrict total video viewing time to less than 20 minutes, sound tapes to no more than 10 minutes
  - use a projection system if there is one – domestic TV screens are very small

- domestic tape recorders are never loud enough so use a sound system
- show large photographs of a tape recording's speakers
- lend tapes to people for private viewing/listening.

- Video camera (CCTV)

  - use it to show fine details of demonstrations, models and diagrams
  - record role plays, etc, for immediate playback to the group
  - record the session for missing students and for your self-review
  - brief the operator about exactly what you want him/her to video.

11 People expect handout material. Take time and trouble to produce good quality handouts as they reflect directly upon your professionalism. Use a consistent type face and layout. If you are reproducing a page from a book, photocopy it once and cut off dirty edge-lines and irrelevant text. Remount this copy on plain paper, 'spot' any remaining marks/splodges with *Tipp-Ex®*, and then use this new 'original' to make multiple copies. Do not put reference dates on your handouts – if you reprint them on another occasion, an old date will be obvious. If you cannot get free photocopying, build the cost into the overall fee. If you have to charge separately, make sure that people are willing to pay and undertake to produce only 'value for money' copies. Consider 72% reductions to double the quantity of printing on an A4 sheet, though always print at 141% on A3 for those with severe visual disabilities. Suggest that friends *might* like to share copies and cost.

12 People seem genetically incapable of passing round even a single pile of handouts without confusion. If you can't give them out personally to each individual, hand just enough along each row rather than the whole stack to the first person. Do not distribute a second one until the first is *well* under way. Get friends to take copies for any absentees. Check everyone has everything before you start teaching. (If you have a very big group, make up

individual sets of coloured and/or numbered handouts and put them in A4 envelopes. Give them out at the start and ask people to take items out as you tell them.)

13 You could use some of the following types of handouts:

- *Summary HOs* include all the important points and main examples.

- *Skeletal HOs* should set out the major points and leave gaps for people to add to as they choose. Reproduce unlabelled or part-labelled graphics for people to complete. (*PowerPoint®* slide print outs are essentially skeletal handouts.)

- *Task HOs* specify the activity you want people to undertake. Add 'Make some notes below' since some people don't like to write on their HOs and then they lose the points they've arrived at.

- *Work books/individual manuals* are usually bound. They allow a student to work at his/her own pace. They are useful for skill learning, especially ICT. (Consider whether you could collaborate with another tutor teaching the same subject and share the authorship and labour.) When your students are using them, monitor their progress and be available to help as required. Independent work support by a work book should not be the only teaching/learning method on offer; bring people together to teach them as a group or subgroup at least some of the time.

- *Article HOs* can reproduce an article in summary form or as the complete text. Give the reference.
- *Reading lists* should be short, user-friendly and annotated. Provide some notes on the main areas covered by each, and indicate the quality and importance of the texts. Say where books can be found: give the library reference codes and bookshop prices. Give the ISBN numbers if there's likely to be any difficulty in locating them.

- *Photographs* can be photocopied quite well though PC digital images reproduce rather better. Build up a collection of picture postcards or cut out pictures from the media and glue them onto card.

- *Questionnaires/quizzes/tests* should be short, made up of none-too-serious items, and written in ways that everyone can achieve some success whatever their level. Use multiple choice items, true/false, diagram labelling, 'what's the question to which this is the answer' as well as closed and open questions. Produce a split half version with answers and ask partners to test each other using 'their half'. Ask pairs to think up a question, write it on a card with the correct answer on the back, then pass it on for others to answer.

14 Many adults feel they ought to take notes and some will actively want to do so. A few will know from past experience that writing notes as they listen helps them structure the information and understand it better – it's one of their preferred ways of learning. People should feel free to make notes if they wish, though listening and participating in the session with you providing the gist in a handout at the end may be the best option for most. Consider:

- *Verbatim note taking*: discourage it. Unless they are taken down in good shorthand such notes are always inaccurate. Writers hardly engage with the material and remember little of what they hear.

- *Analytical note taking*: encourage people to listen and then note down the major points/critical examples in a structured way. You can help people recognise the important points by the way *you* structure what you say and the extra-verbal markers you use (stress, pauses, etc). Make some sample notes and display them on the OHP to give them the idea.

- *Summary note taking*: discourage any note taking but then give 2-3 minutes every quarter of an hour or so for people to put them together, working individually or collaboratively.

Allow them to check with a partner and/or your summary OHP. This procedure promotes analysis, understanding and retention of ideas.

– *Skeletal notes*: provide outline headings and statements on a handout with spaces for students to complete as they wish.

– *Collaborative notes*: suggest that pairs take notes 'one on/one off' over an agreed spell, using carbons or photocopying them afterwards. (Allow time for partners to agree a format/style.)

– *Tape recording*: allow anyone to record the session. Do the same yourself and lend the tape to anyone who wants it, including any absentees. Listen to it yourself and use it to evaluate your presentation. (Video record it as well!)

KEY POINTS

- *Use imaginative teaching resources and AVAs to enhance people's learning and achievement.*
- *Take time and effort to produce good AVAs: they will pay dividends in student interest, motivation, learning and enjoyment.*

---

20 Devising Tasks and Activities

The detail of what students can be asked to do singly, in small groups or as a class, will depend upon the particular subject being studied. However, there are a number of general points about their use that are applicable to most content areas.

1   Whilst it is likely that the nature of a particular task or activity will determine the most appropriate method to use, its purpose must relate to a specific learning outcome. A task/activity can be used either to demonstrate that a learning outcome has been achieved, or as a means of working towards one. 'Students should be able to do X, and working on this task will demonstrate that they can' ... and ... 'If they are to be able to Z, I'll first get them to work on task Y and then help them transfer and build on that learning so that they are able to do Z'.

2   Tasks and activities may be:

   – knowledge based though they can involve practical action eg 'Identify the main causes of the Reformation; Make use of the postcard reproductions to describe the development of imagery.'
   – a practical skill eg 'Draw the four cardboard boxes and show the effects of shadow from a single light source.'
   – based on feelings eg 'Role play a discussion between a parent and a 13 year old daughter about staying out late. Be ready afterwards to describe the arguments made, the outcome and your emotional reactions.'

Tasks and activities can involve the generic actions used for writing learning outcomes – eg interpret, compare, explain – as well as all those behaviours and processes that are specifically related to your subject – eg sketch, measure, decorate, arrange, dribble, design, perform, etc.

3   Write the activity/task down on a handout, flipchart or writing board as well as telling people. You can be sure that someone won't have been attending and will need to be told again. Such information redundancy is helpful, for people often need to check back on exactly what they have been asked to do, or make sure that the feedback they are planning to give is in the correct format. Set out any handout in ways that make it clear where they should write their findings. If you ask for 4 points, provide 4 ltr bullet points or numbered spaces; not only will this give people direction but it will also let you see at a glance how they are progressing. Add 'Make some notes below' so that they then have something to refer back to later. People also need to know:

-   the time available
-   what resources they can use
-   whether they are to make a written summary, give a demonstration, or tell others what they have done
-   how the feedback is to be organised.

4   You can ask students to complete pieces of written work but this is likely to be an individual rather than a collaborative activity. If you set a traditional essay, indicate the likely length, scope, what need there is for 'perfect' English, and any assessment criteria. Remember that some of your group may have problems with literacy and would find such an idea appalling; few of the others are likely to jump for joy at the prospect either. Consider using an alternative, making sure that there is still a good match between what the task/activity asks for and the overall learning outcome(s). You could choose from:

-   a letter to an historical/imaginary/actual person
-   a newspaper article in a particular style ... or in contrasting styles, tabloid vs broad sheet
-   a radio or TV script ... or how a soap and/or a serious documentary might handle the issue
-   an interview transcript with an historical/imaginary/actual person
-   a poem

- a play scene
- a film story-board
- a comic strip
- an autobiographical episode
- a short story
- a book extract 'in the style of ...'

5 There are a number of ways of presenting material to form the basis of tasks and activities. These include:

- artefacts (real and in facsimile)
- case studies
- computerised learning programmes
- diagrams and drawings
- documents (real; in facsimile; historical; contemporary)
- internet material
- media extracts and articles
- *magnetic poetrykits®* aka fridge magnet words
- maps (modern; historical)
- models
- music extracts
- objects
- newspapers and magazines including facsimile historical issues
- radio/TV recordings; CDs and DVDs
- photos
- pictures
- picture postcards
- practical experiments (avoiding the wet and the smelly!)
- reproductions of paintings
- simulations
- specimens.

Printed material can be readily reproduced on a photocopier but be sure that your institution holds a license if you're planning to run off copyright text and images. (NB: Music in copyright may never be reproduced.) Many tasks and activities can be enlivened with – and most handouts enhanced by – illustrations, short text extracts, photographs, maps, etc. A request to 'compare and contrast' becomes much more interesting when it involves visual material; the addition of unidentifiable/historical photographs portraying the characters described make a case study more realistic too.

6   Most of the methods you can use to involve your students in particular tasks and activities, are described in the chapter on managing methods [16]. However, there are a number of quasi methods/resources which may also be useful. These include:

   –   a 'market stall' where items are laid out for examination, identification, dating, comparison, etc.
   –   an 'Antique Road Show' and not necessarily for antiques, but any artefacts, items and objects that lend themselves to such an approach
   –   *Jackdaws*® – a collection of documents, images, photographs, reproductions, maps, etc, relating to a theme (eg 'The Great Fire of London ... The life and times of Hemingway ... Wet land flora and habitats')
   –   toy simulations such as a cardboard grocer's shop, a Victorian cardboard theatre, dolls' house furniture.

What you get people to do and how you get them to do it will depend upon you and how you can enthuse the group to get involved. Be adventurous. A recent session on fakes, forgeries and the darker side of the art world, part of an art history course, was transformed when the tutor switched off the projector and invited the group to commit forgery. Fifteen or so late middle aged, respectable citizens readily distressed photocopies of Hogarth engravings and splashed water, coffee granules, colour wash and salt all over them. They stood back in amazement at their daring and instant achievements, and in the process, recognised how their simulations related to the issues and practices that they had been discussing. If these somewhat staid students wearing their best clothes could be so readily engage in practical activities, then so can yours if you are sufficiently inventive, enthusiastic and encouraging.

7   You may be able to get your students to undertake some work outside the session. Where you do, explain the purpose and discuss with them how important it *actually* is that they do it, the extent to which the next session depends upon everyone completing it, and, in the unlikely event that sanctions are to be invoked for any non-completion, what these are. Homework doesn't have to involve reading and writing, indeed the less formal writing involved, the more likely it is that people will do it! Suggest that they make a short radio item using a tape recorder, take some press cuttings, review a TV programme, interview someone, do a simple experiment, or carry out a social survey of friends or family. If you want them to write something, choose a format from list in *4* above.

8   One valuable way of involving students and increasing active participation in their own learning and in the work of the group, is to have them present/demonstrate something to the rest. When you raise this as a possibility, do so in euphemistic terms, since asking people if they would like 'to volunteer to give a talk to the group' will seem a very risky prospect to many. If however, you suggest 'bringing in something and just saying a bit about it', the idea will seem less threatening. People should be more willing to talk about a personal experience or their understanding of something, within the informality of a 'show and tell' setting.

9   The learning and teaching of your particular subject may focus on individual work and practice, with you providing supervision and feedback. If you teach sports or physical activities, creative subjects, or computer-based topics, then there is the additional issue of who is to decide what an activity/task is to be. Should students always work on their own projects, following particular strands of individual interest or should they work through a series of staged exercises, task and activities which will develop a set of basic/advanced skills? On the other hand, should you exclusively determine what the group is to do – how, when and where – or is there a place for consultation and negotiation about routes, tasks and activities with space for people to follow up their personal projects? It won't surprise you to learn that we would choose a mixed economy, making use of inventive tasks

and activities to provide further opportunities for students to achieve more of their personal goals, more of the time.

KEY POINTS

- *Tasks and activities increase interest, participation and achievement.*
- *Design novel tasks and activities that will both intrigue and motivate people to engage with your subject. Think 'faking Hogarth'.*

IV Reviewing Learning and Teaching

Introduction

Interest in the process and the outcomes of evaluation throughout ACL continues apace. Government agencies, funders, institutions, quality assurance managers, tutors and students have their own good reasons for wanting to find out what is going on in classrooms, and how, and to what effect.

Evaluation as a concept means describing something in appropriate terms and then judging how appropriate or acceptable that something is. The something may be any aspect of education from a total programme to a course or a single session. It encompasses the progress and achievement of individual students, though in the United Kingdom, such an analysis is usually known as *assessment*. Whichever words are used, evaluation has to do with looking at a teaching/learning event with the intention of answering such questions as: 'Is what is being done what was intended? ... Is it being done efficiently and effectively? ... Are the learners achieving something of value?

Evaluation may best be seen as a way of working: a continuous process of observing, analysing and making judgements on the basis of which existing practice can be confirmed and/or changes made. Evidence about a course can be gleaned from a number of sources: the views of course participants, the self-evaluation carried out by a tutor, and the judgment of an external observer. These evaluations will determine the extent to which:

- the aims and learning outcomes are being achieved
- student needs and wants are being met
- the event is value for money and time spent
- the planning, preparation, organisation and management are appropriate
- the tutor exemplifies good adult education practice.

Evidence concerning student achievement can be obtained by both formal and informal methods. Such assessments will determine the extent to which learners have progressed and whether they have achieved subject and/or skill-based learning outcomes, and/or a range of person-related accomplishments.

The following pages suggest ways in which evidence from these several sources can be obtained and interpreted.

21 Attendance and Drop-out

A course attendance record is often held to be a good indicator of what is taking place, how the tutor is working and what the group is achieving. Whilst a significant change in the pattern of attendance over time can signal something is happening, it cannot say what that something is. A number of research studies conducted over the years, often for M.Ed. theses, show that the reasons people attend sporadically, or quit a course altogether, are varied and at least some of them are unrelated to people's actual educational experience. This is not to say that there is no relationship between drop out and quality. Indeed, common sense – and these studies – suggests that there is.

1   Taken as a whole, the data suggest that up to half of the reasons why students drop out of adult education, and about 20% typically do, have to do with what they term 'personal reasons'. The range of issues people cite include competing family demand, work responsibilities, ill health and fatigue, as well as the pull of other interests and hobbies. Personal reasons, however, also include their poor self-confidence as students, what they see as their inability to integrate comfortably into a learning group, and, it has to be said, unsatisfactory aspects of their courses that they still seem unwilling to make explicit.

2   A further quarter of the reasons given reflect people's judgements that the course is not what they expected. In part, this is due to their receiving inadequate pre-course guidance. They may join a course, which, in the event, does not have the approach or subject slant they anticipated or wanted, is pitched at the wrong level, demands a too advanced or too basic level of skill/expertise, or is taught in a way which they feel does not accord with the ways they want to learn.

Part of your responsibilities is to ensure that your courses are described accurately, and to make it clear to people at the first session what the course is about and at what level you expect to work. If you help students establish their needs and starting points, you will also be able to advise them about the appropriateness of the course for their particular needs and aspirations [10]. Amongst other things, you could let them join for the first session as a taster to see whether it is what they want. Your best efforts notwithstanding, people will still enrol with misapprehensions about their own motivation, capabilities, and stamina to stay the course.

3   Up to a quarter of the reasons people give for dropping out relate directly to the tutor, and adult students are perceptive and articulate when they are asked in confidence about the teacher behaviour they find less than acceptable. Criticisms include the inability to cope with content matter or pitch it at an appropriate level, the use of incomprehensible language, poor communication skills, a lack enthusiasm, and an inability – or unwillingness – to relate to people as adults.

4   It is easy to become over sensitive to variations in attendance figures, especially if you teach a long course over a period. All sorts of reasons can be imagined why one or other person hasn't turned up and to assume that there was something in the previous session that you did badly, or that upset them, or seriously prevented their achievement. You may of course be right, but students have an existence beyond adult education and the rest of their lives can sometimes take priority over your course! Consider the following strategies to assuage your insipient guilt:

– agree with your students that where possible, they will try to let you know if they are going to miss a session. You can then save them a handout; or reserve time for them next session; or modify that session so that they will not miss out on a critical piece of learning
– follow up an unexplained or lengthy absence by asking if anyone in the group knows anything; or send a message via a friend; or a postcard; or even make a brief telephone call
– ask the office to contact the student and enquire of their well being and intentions
– ensure that you do find time for them when they reappear.

Ask how they have been and brief them about what they have missed. Negotiate with them about how you can best help them catch up.

5   The fact remains, however, that a high drop-out rate can be saying something significant about the course and/or about you as tutor. If this is the case, then the rest of the group will know what it is. Share your misgivings and concern with those who remain and try to identify not only what the problem(s) is but also how it might be remedied. You may then feel better able to write to those who have dropped out and say that you have had a discussion with the rest of the group, modified the course in such and such a way as a result, and would be delighted to see them if they would like to rejoin you.

6   Having regularly full attendance does not mean that you can assume that your course is problem-free and everyone is completely satisfied. Some quite inept tutors have justified poor teaching practice by claiming that they have full attendance: 'My students are perfectly happy with things as they are ... they wouldn't be here otherwise'. People may be coming because they are loyal to the institution, there is no alternative provision in the subject locally, the equipment is good, or the tutor happens to run a highly competitive resource supply service. One student was heard to say as she left: 'He doesn't get any better, but at least it's warm and the tools are sharp ... and I suppose I do learn something from watching what the rest do, so the time isn't totally wasted!'

7   Carrying out regular course evaluations in a variety of guises and make formal and informal assessments of student progress and achievements will enable you to confirm those aspects of your planning, management and teaching which are working and to modify those which are not. You will also be able to challenge any misuse of your attendance figures, even if they are a bit wobbly at times.

KEY POINTS

- *Give some thought to unexplained drop-outs and what they might be saying about you, the group and/or the course.*
- *Follow up absences sensitively, making it plain to people that you are looking forward to seeing them next time.*

---

22 Course and Session Evaluation

Course and session evaluation should be an ongoing process and not restricted to the end of an event, not least because it is too late at this stage to influence what you have been doing together in any direct way.

1   There are a variety of methods you can employ to evaluate your course using internal observers – your students. The problem is to find out what they *really* think about the course, about themselves as a student group and about you, the tutor. Adults can be very reluctant to voice criticisms publicly. It may be that they remember feeling vulnerable in front of all-powerful teachers at school, and/or they are concerned that you have to make assessments of their work. They may feel unsure of their capabilities as students and perceive the problems they experience are their fault – and they don't want to hurt your feelings either. There is an hierarchy of responses:

  – what they'll tell you in front of other members of the group
  – what they may tell you privately
  – what they'll say within the group during your temporary absence
  – what they'll say to a friend at coffee time or on the way home
  – what they'll say to a partner or a member of their family
  – what they won't tell anyone.

  The skill is to get below the first layer. If you ask too blatantly what they think about you and the course, all you are likely to get are platitudes, and not many of those either. You need to be more subtle!

2   Watch everything that happens before, during and after the session. The cues and clues of people's responses to what you do and what you ask of them are there for you to observe. Whilst body language is not everything, it can provide valuable

indicators. Similarly, the way people say things as well as what they say, the alacrity with which they attempt things, how quickly they leave the room at the end of the session, and so on, will also tell you quite a lot.

3   Get into the habit of listening and talking to individuals from the start of the course. If you are arriving sufficiently early and have prepared everything in good time, you will be free to socialise and chat with people as they come in. There is no reason why you shouldn't initiate some evaluative responses. You could, for example, comment favourably on something a person did and in the course of your conversation ask the student what s/he thought about it and about the session generally – and about a particular piece of teaching or group work you attempted together. You might also say that you did/did not like the way you had done something in the session and enquire what s/he thought about it. (Disingenuous, but it works!) Listen to what people say to each other. Ear-wigging can tell you a lot about what people are thinking and feeling. Don't believe the adage that you'll never overhear anything good about yourself and what you do!

4   You will, however, need to carry out more structured procedures to find out what the group as a whole thinks about the course. You must ask your students at strategic points during a course what they are finding useful and whether there are things they would like modified, and, if so, how? (Too much formal evaluation is left to the last session when it is too late for students opinions to have much effect, at least as far as they are concerned.) One way to do this is by dividing them into small groups and asking them to identify examples of the things they like doing, things they feel are of particular benefit to them and those that they are less keen about. If you also ask them to identify ways in which *the course* might be modified, you will get suggestions that they won't feel are personal criticisms of you. It is important not to expose individuals nor require them to make critical observations too publicly. If you encourage them to work with one or two partners, they will not only feel less vulnerable, but

they will also be able to test out and validate their personal responses and feelings against those of others.

5   Provide opportunities for people to complete some form of paper and pencil report/questionnaire both during the course and at the end. Consider letting people talk the questions through in small groups first and then write their responses.

You can ask open questions, or choose more specific ones, depending on the nature of the group. The most sophisticated formula is: 'Please say anything you like about the course (so far)', though this is one that you will need to be sure your group can handle.

It may be that you judge that they need some indication of the sorts of things you have in mind, so you could extend it as follows: 'Please make some notes of anything you would like to say about the course (so far). You might want to say something about what we have done and/or whether you've enjoyed the course, ways you think it could be improved and how people in the group could contribute to making it more successful. Please write down anything you think I should know, especially if it will help me adapt our course after the break/or the next time I teach it.' Be aware, though, that as soon as you suggest possible areas of response, those are the ones that they are most likely to comment upon.

You might try what appears to be more directed items, though it is the format that appears more straightforward, since they remain open questions, for example:

–   'One of the more useful (valuable) aspects of the course for me is/was ... because ...'
–   'One of the less useful (valuable) aspects of the course for me is/was ... because ...'
–   'The thing(s) I like(d) best about coming on the course is/ was ... because ...'
–   'If I could change the course, I would ... because ...'
–   'I should also like to say that ... because ...'

Notice that it is *more* not *the most, less* not *the least*, and that these questions ask for people's reasons. You need to know *why* people are reacting in the way that they are. Knowing that they do or don't like something doesn't tell you enough; it can't inform your decision about how to change.

If, however, you want specific answers about particular issues, you must ask specific questions. It is no good hoping that they know what you want to know. So ask such things as:

- 'Did you like the small group teaching sessions or would you have preferred to have worked on your own throughout? Please say why.'
- 'What additional resources would you like me to supply?'
- 'How can I make the time I spend with each person fairer all round?'

6 Some tutors (and institutions) employ rating scales including box ticking, multiple choice items, numbers (e.g. 1–10), and words (e.g. excellent; very good, etc). Though these are quick to fill in they don't tell you much. (What would an average of 6.38 really tell you about your communication skills?) If you *are* committed to using them, make sure you use even number response categories – odd numbers result in a tendency to go for the middle point. Include spaces for their reasons and add: 'Why?' or 'Because ...'

One type of rating questionnaire asks students to draw their responses by sketching a smile or a grimace on a face, drawing a picture to represent the course, or ticking a smiley face. Such methods can be of value for students who have limited literacy skills or learning difficulties, but their universal application is doubtful because they can be seen as patronising.

7 Whichever form of paper and pencil questionnaire you use, consider the following:

- Set them out on a sheet with sufficient space for the answers. Take time and trouble to make them look good, indicating by the quality that you judge the procedure – and by implication students' views – to be of real importance.

– You may find it difficult to categorise all the responses that students make to open questions. Burning issues will be obvious but where only a couple of people mention a particular item, it will still be worth thinking their point through to see what they are driving at and why. If one person criticises or commends something, at least two or three others are probably thinking it.

– If you give people the option of anonymity, some may be more candid whilst those who want to own their opinions will give their names. It is certainly more helpful for you as tutor to know who has said what, since it allows you to place the comment in the context of that particular individual and better understand 'where s/he's coming from'.

– If you tell people that you really are interested in what they think and will find their opinions of value in your development as a teacher of adults they will be more willing to take time and trouble in completing an evaluation. Don't blame the management for any imposition of an evaluation process. Not only is it unprofessional but also it implies that you can't see any value in finding out what the group thinks about what you do … and if that's the case, shut this book and give up!

– If you are required to use an evaluation schedule that doesn't tell you want you want to know and you can't get it modified, create your own and ask the group to complete it in addition to the 'official' one.

– Insist on seeing all evaluation sheets completed by your group if the process is controlled by the institution. You have a professional duty to know what your students are saying. A line manager is doing you no favours by withholding formative or summative feedback from you whatever it might be saying about you.

8   You may choose to use open plenary techniques, either in addition to, or instead of paper and pencil methods, where you ask the group to tell you what they think about the course 'up front'. There is a variety of methods you might use: buzz groups, brainstorming, sheets of large paper round the room with a request that people write their comments under headings, *Post-it*® notes grouped together, small groups reporting back to the large group, everyone saying 'one good thing and one less good thing' in the large group, as well as free and open discussion in the large group. Some participants, however, will find these approaches threatening and they are unlikely to be very forthright in what they say; so if you decide that you are going to use these methods, take time to think through the management issues involved, not least of which are:

–   when exactly it should take place and what effect it might have on what else you have planned for the session
–   how you are going to manage it, and whether you should chair it
–   how what they say is going to be recorded
–   how the less articulate are going to be helped to make a contribution
–   what you are physically going to do while it is taking place
–   whether you're going to/should respond to what they say, and if so, how.

9   More formal evaluation activities, whether questionnaire-based or in the plenary group, need to take place at an appropriate time, and the place *not* to undertake them is as the final item! The atmosphere and sense of purpose tail off drastically after an evaluation period, even when the group is feeling very positive about a course. You need to take control of the session after an evaluation is completed and finish on an upbeat, so do it as the penultimate activity – whether it is mid course or end of course event – and then end the session with a bang!

Plenary group techniques *can* be sited during a next-to-last session either before a break or near the course's conclusion. By carrying out the evaluation then, the following/final session can be used to remedy at least one or two of the points raised, give you a chance to say what you think, and to finish on a significant upbeat. (If you are using questionnaires, the group could carry out preliminary small group discussion in the penultimate session, draft their individual responses at home and bring them back for final completion in the last session.)

10 Whichever particular format or combination of formats you use, and whenever you choose to use them, try to remain objective. When people are critical it is difficult not to take it personally. If you are using a group technique, listen quietly to what they have to say and avoid justifying your actions. If you feel you really must explain a particular action or event, try to do so without being defensive. If you are reading people's questionnaires, stay calm. You have, after all, asked for their opinions, and they are giving them out of respect for you. Do not deprecate their approval and praise either; it will have been meant sincerely. Accept and value the confirmation they offer you.

11 Once you know what they have to say, evaluate their evaluations. Make some diagnoses about what they have said and test out some possible explanations. Do their comments seem reasonable? Do they make sense? What is the balance of opinion in the group? Does the original reason you chose to do something still seem justified? Now decide what you are going to do as a result, what changes you are going to make and what practices you feel confirmed in and will use again?

12 The feedback provided by a range of ongoing, more formative evaluations, coupled with knowledge of the extent to which students are achieving specified learning outcomes, will allow you to make modifications to a course as it proceeds. Combine the feedback provided by end-of-course evaluations with what you know about students' learning achievements to plan and improve subsequent courses. The types of evaluation procedures that you use are less important than the fact that you find out what people think about the course both during and at the end of it.

13 Offer the group your evaluation of the course; they'll welcome it. Tell them what you think about what they have achieved and where you think there may have been a shortfall. Comment on the strengths and shortcomings of the course and of your teaching, perhaps giving some indication of what you might do differently another time. Make sure you thank them for their participation … and enthusiasm … and friendship … and sense of group cohesion and support … as well as having taken part in the evaluation processes.

KEY POINTS

- *Begin the on-going process of course evaluation from the very first session.*
- *Use a variety of methods and procedures to identify what is happening; then act on what they tell you while you still can.*

23 Tutor Self-evaluation

An additional and very valuable way of carrying out a course evaluation is for the tutor to do it for him/herself. This not only provides an informed perspective on course planning, structure and content with the attendant student achievement, but it will also help a tutor to reflect upon the development of his/her teaching and management skills.

1   Self-evaluation or self-assessment – the terms in this instance are interchangeable – can be carried out at a number of levels. You can make judgments about how you are working with individual students, how you taught a particular session, and about the strength and weaknesses of your planning, preparation and teaching over a whole course. Self-evaluation can be guided, at least in the early stages, by asking yourself a series of questions about such things as your purposes, planning and preparation, your relationship with the group, your handling of the content, the choice and management of the methods you use, the ways you assess learning and achievement, and so on. Subsequently you may wish to concentrate on one or two aspects in turn.

2   Some appropriate questions are given below but they are by no means all-inclusive. Indeed, the questions themselves are less important than the habit of thinking about your work as a teacher of adults, so you can confirm your good practice and modify those aspects that require change.

- Do I respect my students as adults and meet them on equal terms ... and ...

    - do I demonstrate a commitment to equal opportunities in the way I work?
    - do I create a friendly, informal and welcoming atmosphere, treating each student as an individual and using his/her name?

- do I make it apparent that I have time for people, especially or those who do not like to speak in front of others or who may want to discuss a private matter?

• Do people feel confident and at ease within the group ... what have I done to promote it ... and ...

- do I encourage them to contribute their experience and expertise, valuing what they offer, yet challenge any errors?
- does everyone get the opportunity to participate and offer their experience and opinions, or just the more articulate and able ones?
- do I avoid all discriminatory practices?

• Do I show a willingness to negotiate as well as consult the group ... and ...

- have I consulted them on those things on which I need to take the decision?
- have I discussed and agreed with the group at the start of the course those things that we can negotiate?
- am I sure that what we do and how we do it continues to be agreeable to the group and not just what I want and/or think we should be doing?

• Am I clear about the aims and learning outcomes for the course and for each session, and do my planning, preparation and teaching take full account of them ... and ...

- do students know what their starting points are ... and do I?
- do my students know what they are trying to achieve at any given point ... and are their needs being met?
- who sets the standards they are expected to reach? When I do, is it clear to them at what level they are to achieve ... and when they set them, do I know what they are?

- Have I prepared appropriate material at the right level to provide the group with what they need to know and be able to do ... and ...

  - do I know my material sufficiently well and have I thought through the order and structure of what I propose to do?
  - do I present material step-by-step in short units ... relate new content and ideas to what they already know, using appropriate examples ... and involving them and facilitating their participation?
  - do I have a range of different tasks, activities and learning materials to accommodate the different needs and starting points of individuals?

- Do I use a range of methods ... and have frequent changes of activity during the session ... and ...

  - do I choose techniques and procedures that accord with people's preferences?
  - do I use audio visual aids and other learning resources when and where they will help people's learning?
  - do I make a task quite clear, then sensitively monitor what people are doing, valuing the results and making subsequent use of them?

- Am I fair in allocating my time and attention to individuals, when they are working on their own ... and ...

  - do I first listen and find out what the student thinks about his/her progress?
  - do I diagnose and assess the difficulties individuals are facing and, once knowing what they are, help in sympathetic and constructive ways?
  - when I leave, does an individual feel satisfied with our discussion ... and know what to do next ... and feel motivated to do it?

- Do I give the group plenty of opportunities to say what they are achieving and what they think about the session and the course ... do I listen ... and ...

    - am I clear about what has been achieved during a session and the extent to which the session's learning outcomes have been attained?
    - do I provide people with diagnoses, feedback and confirmation of their work, even though they don't like to call it assessment
    - do I ensure that the group and individuals leave with a sense of having accomplished something worthwhile and have a desire to learn more?

- Do I demonstrate an enthusiasm for my subject, my teaching and my students ... and ...

    - are the people in my group motivated, responsive, confident, hard working and full of initiative?
    - do I always remember that it is the learning and achievement of my students that are all important, not my teaching?
    - do I enjoy what I do and do I do it well? If I do, what am I going to do to further my professionalism and sense of satisfaction? If I don't, what am I going to do about it?

KEY POINTS

- *Get into the habit of reflecting upon each session as to what you did and what the group achieved.*
- *Check your self-evaluations against other evidence. You may sometimes be too self-critical*

---

24 Assessing Student Learning and Achievement

Assessment is concerned with the sampling of some aspect of a person's behaviour at a particular moment. Depending upon the kind of sample taken, inferences can be drawn about that person's achievements, abilities, motivation, aptitudes, and so on. These inferences can in turn be used to diagnose a student's strengths and weaknesses, offer him/her feedback about how s/he is doing, sustain a sense of motivation and interest, and provide recognition of achievement and progress. By indicating whether the learning outcomes have been achieved, assessment can also provide evidence about the strengths and shortcomings of the course.

Where assessment is used to identify areas of strengths and weaknesses, potential ability or aptitude, it is described as being diagnostic. Where assessment takes place during a learning sequence and is used to provide feedback to the student about how s/he is progressing towards a desired end, it is described as being formative. Where assessment is used to measure the extent of the learning that has taken place by the end of a sequence, it is described as being summative.

How assessments of student learning are actually made can range from the most informal to the highly formal – from watching and listening to students as they work to an end-of-programme final examination. The crucial feature of assessment is what it tells the student and the tutor, and how both make use of that information.

1   As you work with a group of adults, you are likely to be making constant and seemingly intuitive judgments about the effects of what you are doing. Thus you may identify at a given point that most students seem to have grasped the idea and that you can move on, or that few seem able to handle the material properly and you must stop and give them more discrete practice. This valuable set of monitoring and evaluative skills provides you with the feedback you need to decide what you should do from one section to the next. Whilst this informal 'aggregate' assessment

of the group's progress is critical, it still has to be complemented by assessments of each individual. You need to know what every member of the group is doing and the extent to which they are meeting the course and their own learning outcomes. Only then can you decide what and how to teach the next segment to the group as well as providing the differentiated help and guidance that individuals need.

2   Many adults have a marked aversion to assessment, or at least to what they believe it to be. A study of adult students in a variety of ACL[1] settings shows that they have an antipathy to the language and concept of 'Assessment' with a big *A*: 'Knowing you are learning is more important than proving it'. They believe that feedback is quite different to assessment for they equate assessment with summative testing and grading, rather than seeing it as being a diagnostic and formative process. Nevertheless they *are* clear that the tutor's role is to:

–   help with technical and practical problems
–   provide confirmation of learning gain
–   provide feedback and constructive criticism
–   affirm and encourage ...

which is somewhat ironic as these are *all* component features of any assessment process. In addition to their perceptions of what assessment should and shouldn't be, many adult students also lack confidence in themselves as learners and any public identification of on-going achievement – and especially of failure – will not be welcomed, even within the safe confines of the group. They will have humiliating memories from their schooling, and their expectation is that they should now be treated as adults and not as children.

3   If you take a low-key approach to assessment, it becomes an integral part of learning and teaching. Instead of appearing as

[1] Turner, C and Watters, K *'Proof Positive. Students views of the approaches to identifying achievement in non-accredited learning.* NIACE, 2001

'testing to find out what I don't know', it becomes an on-going monitoring of progress and achievement, with feedback 'keeping me informed on how I'm doing and what to do next'.

Fortuitously – and who would have guessed it – the participatory activities that we have mentioned so often in this book not only give people opportunities to manipulate and use ideas, information and skills to promote permanent and transferable learning, but they also allow students and tutors to recognise and evaluate ongoing learning gains. So as you design and run your courses, build in some of the following procedures that will help both you and your students to judge their learning and progress:

- Student presentational activities:
    - giving a short talk to the class
    - reading/acting out an excerpt
    - giving a demonstration to the class
    - showing and telling to the class
    - feedback from and comment on small group work
    - offering explanations, examples, relevant anecdotes, etc

- Student shared activities:
    - working on tasks in small group
    - taking part in class discussions
    - taking part in peer assessment of each others' work
    - contributing to a class project
    - acting out a situation using role play or simulation
    - carrying out activities on a field trip/visit

- Student individual activities:
    - answering questions
    - asking questions
    - undertaking critical reading
    - producing a piece of written work
    - working on a personal task/project
    - using primary materials
    - completing work sheets, manuals, etc
    - using computer generated programmes

- carrying out practical work
- undertaking an individual study or project
- keeping a log or diary
- making notes/using handouts
- doing a test/quiz/questionnaire
- using/making a sound tape or video
- undertaking a private visit/field trip
- doing tasks and activities at home.

As tutor, you are working to facilitate student learning, so look for positive change in the way individuals – and the group – think and act as they handle new knowledge, ideas and skills. Do the *quality* of answers given, comments made, tasks completed, etc, indicate any advancement in thinking, skill or understanding over time? Is there a positive change in the use and handling of subject language, examples offered, explanations given, connections made, or transfers achieved? Are they (now) using the correct tool in the right way; are their movements more supple; is their use of colour more appropriate? Making use of the evidence from a range of participatory tasks and activities will allow both you and each student to make judgements about the learning being achieved as well as providing a basis from which you can offer formative feedback.

4 In addition to the embedded activities suggested above, you can also use other subject-specific techniques that will tell you and your students about their achievements without putting them on the spot. Amongst other things you could ask people to:

- complete a task/activity which, whilst similar to that which they have been working on, is sufficiently different to identify whether they can transfer what they have learnt
- work together and give each other feedback
- work together and prepare a routine to show to others
- identify the salient points of/solve a case study
- carry out a problem-solving/practical task
- draw up some guidelines for 'someone just starting out'
- role play a situation and observe/learn from each other

- fill in the blanks ... complete a diagram ... spot the mistakes
- undertake a piece of homework to apply what has been learnt.

5   When you offer formative feedback to an individual about what s/he has achieved, you need to strike a balance between objectivity and frankness on the one hand and a recognition of an individual's stage of current development, potential level of achievement on the other. A student will have a pretty fair idea of what s/he has done, and s/he wants your honest appraisal, confirmation and guidance. The knowledge of a student's starting point will allow you to target your feedback in individually appropriate and sensitive ways.

6   When you are working in a one-to-one situation, you have the further advantage of being able to find out more exactly what the student thinks about his/her achievement. You can ask direct questions aimed at uncovering perceived strengths and weaknesses. You can try to discover whether s/he fully understands a particular point, or if s/he feels confident about performing a particular skill before s/he shows you. The need for sensitivity remains paramount. The conversational approach will encourage greater candour, and whilst the positive feedback and encouragement you offer should result in achievement and progress, be aware that a careless comment can prove demoralising. (One of the authors was recently a student on a beginner's painting course. As the tutor began to appraise a first attempt at watercolour, he commented that the brand of paper used was a particularly good choice since it could be taken into the shower, washed off and used a second time!)

7   When you make informal assessments on a one-to-one basis, you should:

- give the student your full attention
- remember to use her/his name
- make eye-to-eye contact, smile and look friendly
- take care that your discussion is as private as it reasonably can be

- find out what the student thinks about her/his achievement first
- confirm positive self-evaluations but do not collude with false self-deprecations
- reinforce positive aspects (and say 'Good' in one of 37 ways)
- limit the amount of criticism you offer
- use language that will be understood
- relate your assessments to the individual's previous work, rather than to that of others in the group
- discuss with the student what s/he should do next
- be specific in any guidance or advice you provide
- ensure that the expectations agreed between you are achievable
- reaffirm the one or two features that the student is to work on
- finish on a positive note and thank the student
- find an opportunity to reassess and give further confirming feedback.

8 Students should be encouraged to form opinions about their own work and learn to trust their own judgements. Talking with them on a one-to-one basis about their achievements is one way of helping them develop these skills, though all forms of assessment should encourage and make use of people's self-evaluations. The more practice they have in making judgments of their own work against the yardsticks you provide, the better they will be able to assess their own achievements when they are working on their own.

9 Some tutors make use of peer assessment. Students show their on-going – and finished – work to the rest of the group, discuss what they are doing, what they think about it, and invite others to comment. This can be done in an art exhibition format at the end of a session or as a short show and tell at any time. Once people have got used to the idea, they are usually very positive about it. They learn from what others have to say, they learn by looking and commenting on the work of colleagues, and they develop a sense of constructive self-criticism, of self-confidence and of self-regard.

10 There will be occasions when more formal assessment procedures are called for. You may need to check people's understanding, skill and progress before they exhibit or perform in public, take an outside examination or move to an advanced group. You will know the techniques common to your particular subject area and you should discuss the procedure to be used with the group. Negotiate as much of it with them as you can. Make sure they understand why you are suggesting they should attempt it, and agree the way that the results are to be handled and fed back to individuals. Once individuals are fully aware of the purposes of the assessment, the procedure, and any consequences of taking or not taking part, the choice must remain theirs whether or not to undertake it.

An afterword ...

In the wider context of education, training and employment, the radical shift in the manner in which achievement is assessed and recorded continues. A number of factors have contributed to the debate. These include:

–   Government's concern to provide a trained/retrained adult workforce possessing readily transferable qualifications
–   the recognition of significant numbers of citizens who for one reason or another, remain beyond educational and training provision, many of whom are functionally illiterate and innumerate
–   the need by the government and other funding agencies to undertake quality assurance of provision
–   the debate amongst employers, professional groups and educational institutions about the relevance and appropriateness of current training for the workplace
–   the desire for a unified qualification structure (or at least comparable set of structures) which describes levels of attainment
–   the concern of educators and of students themselves for a more user-friendly system which focuses on individual needs rather than institutional demands, one moreover which eases transferability of learning credit and the accreditation of prior learning

– the need to establish an acceptable-to-all procedure which will recognise student achievement in what was previously called non-vocational learning, which includes that tranche of ACL provision which is specifically designed not to be formally accredited.

Whilst an acceptable all-embracing resolution is yet to be put in place, progress is being made. The areas currently being worked on include: a unified set of levels from a pre entry level of basic literacy and numeracy to that of university higher degrees, the reorganisation of responsible bodies for professional and vocational standards, greater comparability in both standards and the demands of awarding bodies and the influence of the Qualification and Certification Authority (QCA), and the development of a staged process which recognises and records achievement in non accredited provision. Whatever the final detail, it does seem likely that a more holistic picture of individuals will be one of the results. Not only should this provide government and funding agencies with more of the evidence they need, but also be of greater value to the individual adult student him/herself, and to the community as a whole.

Keep abreast of the developments in the assessment and recording procedures in your particular sector. It is in your interests as well as those of your students that you are fully aware of the modification and changes that will affect their learning and your teaching.

KEY POINTS

- *Assess your students' progress and achievements continuously so that you – and they – can identify how they are doing and what they are to do next.*
- *Find out what the student thinks about what s/he has done before you offer your judgements in sensitive and constructive ways.*

25 Observing Teaching and Learning – Being Visited

It cannot have escaped the notice of any tutor working in the public sector where some or all of the funding comes from government sources, that the quality of the education provided, the standards achieved, and the efficiency of resource management are of major interest. Even where funding comes from charitable and/or private foundations, there is still a concern for such quality assurance (QA), in essence, that students are learning and progressing in the ways intended.

Though many ACL and other educational agencies already had quality assurance procedures in operation, it was the establishment of the Common Inspection Framework (CIF) by the Adult Learning Inspectorate (ALI), and the Office for Standards in Education (OFSTED) that proved the major watershed. Hereafter, practically every ACL provider brought its QA procedures – and particularly the observation of teaching and learning within the classroom (OTL) – into line with the CIF methodology. Though the CIF has been modified (2005) and the inspectorates combined, it remains essentially the same, not least in its view that the heart of the quality assurance process is observation of teaching and learning (OTL) in the classroom.

This chapter is concerned with the process of OTL as seen from the tutor's point of view, and since the CIF procedure is so influential and widespread, we have taken it as the basis of our main description.

1   Evidence of what is going on in the classroom, and how, and to what effect, can be gathered from tutors' reports, students' course evaluations and self-assessments, accredited results and other external achievements, progression routes, and even from registers. Independent observation of teaching and learning offers direct verification. With thorough training of observers, their use of agreed criteria, and the moderation of their judgements, OTL results in valid and reliable portrayals of learning and teaching.

2 The CIF is concerned with *How effective and efficient is the provision of education and training in meeting the needs of learners, and why?* The key questions that guide inspection are:

- *Achievement and standards*
  1 How well do learners achieve?
- *The quality of provision*
  2 How effective are teaching, training and learning?
  3 How well do the programmes and activities meet the needs and interests of students?
  4 How well are learners guided and supported?
- *Leadership and management*
  5 How effective are leadership and management in raising achievement and supporting all learners?

Observation of teaching and learning in the classroom, as well as the inspection of an institution, are awarded overall grades on a four point scale:

1 Outstanding	2 Good	3 Satisfactory	4 Inadequate

3 The focus of session observation is ensuring that learning is taking place and that the learner is at the heart of the learning process. Amongst other things, it looks at:

- *how well students are achieving, ie*
  - success in achieving challenging targets, including qualifications and learning goals (ie LOs)
  - standards of learners' work in relation to the LOs
  - learners' progress relative to their prior attainment and potential
  - the development of personal and learning skills

- *how effective are teaching, training and learning, i.e.*
  - how well teaching and training meets individuals needs

and course/programme requirements (including planning, methods, teaching styles, resources, accommodation, equality of opportunity, etc.)
- the suitability and rigour of assessment and monitoring of progress
- the diagnosis of/provision for additional learning needs

- *how the programme/activities meet the needs and interests of students, i.e.*
  - matching students' aspirations and potential, and building on prior attainment and experience

- *how well students are guided and supported, i.e.*
  - safeguarding welfare, promoting personal development and the achievement of high standards
  - in relation to courses, programmes and career progression
  - contributing to staying safe and healthy.

4   If you have read this far, you will have recognised that the concerns of OTL *à la* CIF, accord exactly with what has been suggested throughout this book. There is little here that you haven't read about in the preceding pages, and, it is to be hoped, are already putting into practice.

   In thinking about what you need to do and how you need to do it, recognise that whilst you are a significant player in any OTL, the observer – inspector or quality assurance manager – is concerned with every thing that is happening in the classroom and it is your students as much as you who are the focus, namely: are they learning ... are they achieving ... are they making progress? You must therefore provide a range of opportunities for them to make clear that they are doing so.

5   Your institution will brief you about its own procedures for an external inspection or internal QA visits; what follows here are some suggestions that should apply across the board.

   - Advise the group of what is to take place. Neither you nor they can refuse a visit, so it is a matter of information rather than a seeking of permission. Anticipate their 'collusion against the outsider'. Though they may initially be subdued, they will be supportive, responding positively to what you ask and they will try to show themselves – and you – in a positive light *if you give them the opportunities to do so*.

– Expect courtesy but reserve from an OTL visitor; whilst they will behave in a friendly manner, they won't join in the session or comment publicly. They will introduce themselves briefly, then sit at the back or to the side and observe quietly. Expect that they'll take notes, though there is no correlation between how much they write and their judgements – some keep running descriptions, others prefer bullet points.

– Provide the observer with a course outline, a session plan and any handouts that you plan to use as a minimum. You *should* have a course file that also includes a brief description of the course context and of students' backgrounds, a scheme of work, previous session plans plus your evaluations so far, previous handouts used, records of students' work and achievements. You might also include a 'What Next' sheet.

– If your students have undertaken tasks, activities, individual or group projects, ask them to bring them in so that the observer can review what they have been doing.

6   You will have planned and prepared thoroughly, so the session to be observed should be relatively easy to manage and teach. You can expect to be anxious, some tutors more so than others, but this can soon turn into a desire to show what you and your students can do. The acid test of a session is whether the learning outcomes have been met, i.e. what students have achieved, and whether they have been appropriately challenged, in line with the overall course programme. It follows then, that what needs to be observable during a session includes:

- early clarification of the session purpose and learning outcome(s) in ways that allow students to fully understand what is involved
- the ways that the session relates to a previous one(s)
- management of the session, of time, of the group and of individuals
- active involvement and engagement of students, with use being made of their contributions, existing knowledge and experience
- use of appropriate methods and learning opportunities/activities in relation to LOs
- evidence of risk assessment, attention to H and S, and the appropriateness of the venue
- effective use of appropriate resources, handouts and AVAs
- motivation of students and the meeting of their individual needs
- most critically of all, however, is the need for clear evidence of student learning, achievement and progress. This means that you *must* provide opportunities for the demonstration of such learning gain as part and parcel of the session's teaching and learning activities.

7 Expect that the observer will want to talk with you about the session and what s/he observed. If this meeting cannot take place immediately afterwards, then it must follow within a day or two, and the feedback should be formative as well as summative. It *might* be restricted to the observer giving you his/her view of what took place, though it ought to be a two-way discussion as this is an important opportunity for you to talk with an informed adult educator about what you are doing. S/he will certainly want to say something about the planning/teaching decisions you made and the ways you worked, as well as identifying the strengths and weaknesses of your teaching and of your students' learning. You, in your turn, can respond to his/her judgements, and seek guidance about alternative strategies.

If you didn't quite manage to do what you detailed in your session plan then the observer will be interested in your reasoning for changing tack, deciding to continue with an activity beyond the planned time or whatever. Teaching is full of critical incidents that require flexibility; such actions aren't necessarily shortcomings and few sessions go exactly according to plan.

If the visit is part of an 'internal' QA procedure, you should subsequently receive a report summarising what you discussed together and detailing the session's strengths and weakness, an overall grade and suggestions for future action.

8   There are two variants of OTL where CIF interests are not paramount. The first is where you, the tutor, are part of a continued professional development (CPD) tutor training course. The major purpose of OTL in this context is formative: to confirm your existing good practice, to help you modify any weaknesses, and to enhance/develop your skills, approaches and course management. It is about moving tutors through a phased development from 'beginner', dependent upon external goals and concerned with surviving and acquiring a bag of tricks, through to a 'fully functioning' professional, able to improvise, experiment and cope with the ambiguities that arise in teaching adults[2].

9   A second OTL variant is informal peer visiting whereby you invite another tutor to act as an observer of one of your sessions and you visit his/hers. You agree what should be looked at, including those aspects that you'd particularly like some feedback about, and then together discus his/her observations after the visit. Considerable benefit can be derived from this informal procedure, not least because by attending his/her session, you can pick up techniques and ideas for use on your own course, as well as developing your skills of observing and assessing. If you decide to try this out, consider the following:

–   It isn't imperative that your colleague teaches the same subject unless you especially want comment about how you handle particular content or specialised methods. Good adult teaching transcends the subject taught and a view from

[2] Gregorc AF. *'Developing Plans for Professional Growth'*. NASSP Bulletin 1973 Dec. pp. 1–8.

someone working in another area can throw fresh light on what you do.

– Explain to your students what you are proposing and secure their agreement. If they don't like the idea, you should respect their views, though it is unlikely that they will be anything but supportive.

– Rather than discussing the session immediately afterwards, you could meet a day or so later when you both have had time to reflect on what took place. Make some notes yourself and compare your self-assessment with your colleague's judgement. Try to avoid feeling defensive or threatened by what s/he may say. When you are the observer, listen carefully to what the tutor says so that you can frame your contributions sensitively. Confirm good practice as well as offering constructive criticism.

– Give your group some feedback about what your visitor had to say and what you discussed together. Pass on any compliments. Use the opportunity to find out about what the group thinks about the course by asking them if they agree with the points the two of you talked about.

10 As a tutor you should see mainstream OTL less as a 'spy in the cab' and more as an opportunity for you to gain feedback, constructive criticism, confirmation and encouragement of what you are doing and what your students are achieving.

KEY POINTS

- *OTL is an opportunity for you to confirm how you and your students are doing. Welcome it.*
- *Strive to make all the sessions you teach – and the student achievement that result – at least as good as the ones that are observed.*

V Getting Started

Introduction

All the preparation and planning in the world can't put off the inevitable. There comes the time and place when the tutor and adult students meet to teach and to learn!

This final section brings together many of the points made elsewhere in the book, and places them in the immediacy of a first session. We also have also included three areas of on-going concern for many tutors; self-presentation or communication skills, coping with difficult students, and providing students with suggestions for progression. If this isn't enough, there is a cake-frosting finale of 'highly practical points' as a summary.

26 The First Session

What a tutor does at the beginning of a session, whether it is the first of a sequence, or a one-off event, critically affects what happens next.

1   An effective beginning has to do with:
    – gaining people's attention and creating interest in what is to follow
    – helping them settle down, relax, and feel at ease with one another and with you the tutor
    – setting the expectations and tone for the rest of the session
    – establishing a climate conducive to learning and achievement.

    The last few minutes of a session are important for:
    – helping students to consolidate what they have learned
    – motivating them to continue their learning (and return next week)
    – finding out what they think about the session and what they have achieved.

2   The first session with any new group of adults is a testing occasion for new and experienced tutors alike. Unless course members have worked together before, they are likely to lack confidence in themselves, feel ill at ease in the company of other participants and may even doubt the wisdom of having joined the course at all. There is nothing very surprising about these anxieties, though it is important that you help them get over such feelings quickly, and they quite rightly look to you to aid this process. Some of the strategies, which will help you – and them – are outlined below.

3   Arrive in plenty of time, make yourself known to the centre staff, find out their names and use them. Administrative staff and caretakers are important people in any establishment and you can be sure you will have need of their help and support! Check

that there are no last minute room or timetable changes, administrative requests, alterations in the enrolment procedures, and whether there is to be a fire practice. Locate the resources store, photocopier, and so on, and find out the procedure for using them. Establish if and when refreshments are available, and where the emergency exits and nearest lavatories are to your teaching room so that you can give this information to the group. In truth, most of this preparatory work is *much* better done on a preliminary visit. You will feel much more at ease as you arrive for a first session if you know the staff, where you're going, and what you have to contend with (see [14]).

4   Inspect your teaching room. If materials have been left out by previous occupants, tidy them away. Draw a quick map of the room so that you can put things back where you found them.

   –   If the room is not suitably arranged for the sort of work that you are going to do, change it. Avoid straight rows of chairs and tables; a curved shape is usually much better. Consider whether to rotate the room through 90° and work lengthwise. Tables may not be needed at all, though some students do prefer the security they offer. If you need a table to work from, then put your chair to the side, rather than behind. Even if the group is to be physically active throughout the session, place chairs round the sides of the room so that they have somewhere to sit and leave their belongings when they first arrive. Match the number of chairs and/or work stations to the expected number of students. In case one or more of your students have a physical disability, be ready to adapt the layout once you have discussed with them what they prefer. Adjust the heating, lighting and ventilation. Put a sign on the door.

   –   Check that all the equipment you need is there, that you know how to use it and it works. Position things in such ways that everyone will be able to see and/or hear. If you need to use a piece of equipment part way through the session, mark its position on the floor with chalk, then put it to one side in an easily accessible place. Lay out your materials and notes in order so that they are available in the sequence you need them. Clean any writing boards, put a fresh sheet of paper on the flip chart and clean the lenses of the OHP. If you are using a laptop and digital projector early on, boot up and leave it set ready to go on with a dark screen saver.

– When you have finished your preparation, check round the room to see that it looks neat, safe, purposeful and welcoming. It will help set the tone for the session and people will notice the results of your efforts as they come in. Some tutors play quiet mood music, and if it seems appropriate to do so, you could too.

5 Since you will be fully prepared and ready to go before anyone arrives, you are free to greet people as they arrive. Introduce yourself to each one as s/he comes in, smile, and ask for their names and use them! Listen to what people have to say, as they may well give you clues about themselves, their interests and their experience. Introduce people to one another so that they can chat together. Try not to get buttonholed by an over-talkative individual at the expense of new arrivals.

6 Prepare a set of name badges beforehand if you have an enrolment list. You will have to decide which names you are going to use, though for most ACL settings first names are the most appropriate. Use a dark, permanent, felt-tipped pen and print large enough so that you can read them at a distance. Wear one yourself and hand them to people as they arrive. If you don't have a list, ask people what they would like to be known as and write badges for them. (If they are to do their own, ensure they use your big pens and that they write in large letters.) If you are using tables, you might also prepare table nameplates by folding pieces of A4 card into a stapled, *Toblerone*® shape. Write the names on all three sides so that however they fall they are readable, not least by those sitting along side. Do something similar for an ICT group, by placing names on top of each VDU. Remember to take the badges and nameplates home with

you for use next time – and every time. This way, they'll not be forgotten.

7 When the majority of people have arrived – and certainly not later than five minutes beyond the published starting time – begin.

– Your physical position in relation to the group is important in helping to gain their attention and communicate with them. Most tutors prefer to stand, while others feel more comfortable sitting down. One or two even kneel! There are no hard and fast rules, but remember to make sure that everyone can see and hear you, that you can see each of them, and that you don't encroach on their personal space.

– Your choice of words and the personal manner in which you begin are also important. However lacking in confidence you might feel, you need to appear friendly, welcoming and quietly enthusiastic. Maintain direct eye contact with people, and sweep the group with your gaze so that you include each person in what you are saying.

– Announce that you would like to start but don't do so until you have everyone's attention. Introduce yourself by name and, if you want to, give a brief description of who you are and your interest in the course topic.

8 Some tutors like to start a session with icebreakers. They feel that these social group techniques promote the integration of individuals and help a group to gel. This may be true, but many adults, especially those new to adult education, may be rather startled by their use. Unless you feel confident that the circumstances are right, it would be wise to avoid the more lengthy or extravagant of these activities.

Nevertheless, it is a very good idea to help people to get to know each other. One useful procedure, especially for larger groups, is for you to pose some general questions about previous experience, back ground, and so on, and ask for a show of hands. Another non-threatening method for smaller groups is to ask people to say who they are, where they come from plus one or two things about their interest in the subject. This can be done first in pairs or trios then relayed to the group by the individual or by a partner. (You could draw yourself a simple seating plan as they report back and make a note of any relevant information, but don't forget to look at them as they speak and thank each one by name when they finish.)

9   Whether or not you begin with such activities, you must to decide if you are going to get started on some aspect of the course content straight away or deal with the administrative and organisational items. You will have to do both at some stage; some vital issues *must* be dealt with straight away – emergency exits; workshop safety; break and finishing times, etc – but the majority can usually be left until the session is well underway.

Our practice is to get on with some content proper as soon as possible and engage people with a topic, for this is why they have come and what they want. Make the opening colourful and lively. Use an AVA, an anecdote or a subject chestnut as part of a brisk opening to create interest and spark motivation. Then if you can, use a non-threatening activity that will allow the group to actively participate. Give small groups something to examine, analyse or interpret, then seek their judgements after they have had some time working together. In the process of their discussions they will learn something *and* begin to get to know each other. Subsequent consultations about the course and what you propose will be more effective as a result of this initial task-based activity. People will be more willing to say what they think about your ideas, and to describe their needs and starting points, once they have rolled their sleeves up and discovered they aren't quite so ignorant and that they've already learnt something about the subject.

10 Towards the end of the session, take time to discover what your students think about what you have done together and what they feel they have learnt. Summarise what *you* think has been covered, and say something about their achievements. Confirm any arrangements that have been agreed regarding the

organisation and procedure of subsequent sessions, and say what you hope will be covered next time, accentuating the potentially enjoyable and rewarding features. Remind them of anything they have to do or bring with them next time.

Make it easy for people to clarify any general queries that they might have about the course, though tell them that they can speak with you afterwards if there is anything they would like to follow up individually. Thank them for their interest and attendance, and say that you have enjoyed working with them and look forward to seeing them again.

11   Get into the habit of 'first in, last out', not just on the first session but every time – another of the very few 'musts'! Staying behind gives you the opportunity to pack away your materials and resources and to ensure that the room is back in its original layout. It also gives individuals the space to speak with you on their own or in a small group. At this stage, people can have a variety of personal issues to which they want answers: they may want to confide in you, be reassured that they will be able to cope, have a particular learning need, or want to tell you that they'll have to miss a future session. You can learn a great deal about individuals, their problems, goals and likely progress, and at the same time gain useful feedback about your teaching and session management so far. Once everyone has left, start thinking about the how the session went, what was achieved and what you need to do next time. Remember to make a note of your conclusions on your session plan.

KEY POINTS

- *How you present and manage the first few minutes of a session will set the tone of what is to follow and how it will be received.*
- *How you end a session and talk with people afterward will affect their motivation to achieve and to return.*

27 Self-presentation

The ways in which tutors present themselves and actually say things are important communication skills. The tutor is the focus of attention much of the time and, whether we like it or not, our message is affected not only by how we structure and phrase what we say but also how we present it, verbally, non-verbally and extra-verbally.

1   There are few 'musts' in adult teaching, but making eye contact with the adults in front of you is one of them. If you don't, people will think you are unsure, uninterested, and shifty. 'Sweep the room' constantly and make eye contact with everyone, taking care not to miss out those seated at the sides. Avoid concentrating on the person who looks particularly friendly or especially interested, and steer clear of addressing a fixed point above their heads and that includes the clock!

   Meeting each person's gaze for two or three seconds indicates that you are interested in him/her as an individual, and you want his/her continued attention. If you have to talk with one person for a period, your mutual eye contact will increase, but don't forget to look round the rest of the group to show that you remain interested in them too, and that they should be listening to what is being said.

2   Speak at a speed that matches the understanding of the group and the complexity of the material. Large rooms and big groups generally require a slower pace than might be anticipated. Changing your pace to a slightly faster delivery can excite and stimulate, whilst using a slower speed can dramatise and emphasise what you are saying. But whatever your pace, enunciate clearly. Project your voice, speak firmly, confidently and audibly without being overloud or too dominant. Ask people if they can hear should you have any doubts, but by constantly looking at people, sweeping the room to make eye contact, your voice should automatically adjust to what is required. (Should a microphone really be needed, use a clip-on radio microphone to avoid being tied to one spot.)

3   Extra-verbal signals indicate what is important. Your inflexion, tone, vocal emphasis and use of pauses will all serve to aurally underline what you are saying, separate it from the main message or even signal a throw-away line that is not to be taken too seriously. Remember that some members of your group may not be users of English as a first language, and extra-verbal cues, as well as verbal nuances, may be missed. Take care that what you intend to be understood, is indeed understood.

   Control verbal tics – 'Er', 'OK?', 'You know?' It is embarrassing to discover that the group is running a sweepstake on how many times per hour you clear your throat or say 'Um'!

4   There is a lot of nonsense talked about movement and gesture. Use both with verve; they are valuable communication devices. Gestures can underline a point, describe an object or action, and illustrate an emotion, whilst movement adds dynamism and interest. Be yourself and don't feel overly constrained.

   –   Take up a position in front of the group so that you can be seen by everyone but without appearing dominant. (A low dais *may* be helpful but unless you have to work formally using presentational methods, they are to be avoided.) Create and maintain an open space in which you feel free to move but avoid encroaching on the personal space of those nearest to you. If they are seated and you are standing, their psychological comfort zone is much less than yours, so don't crowd them. If you need a table, stand or sit to the side. You will appear more open to the audience and you can still lay out your materials. Better still, work in front of it! (If you *must* use a lectern, at least come out from behind it from time to time.)

   –   Make full use of your teaching zone. Your movement will help maintain interest not least because you will appear inclusive of those on the other side of the room, and it will encourage people to change their seated posture as they follow you with their eyes. Avoid marathon walks and caged animal pacing though!

– An open body attitude is to be preferred. An upright stance, holding your arms slightly away from your body will suggest openness, sincerity and conciliation, whilst folded arms can indicate rigidity or impatience. Standing severely erect with crossed hands in front of you may suggest uncertainty and nervousness; a more relaxed posture can signal approachability, belonging and encouragement. When you're sitting, lean forward as this suggests interest and a readiness to engage; loll back (with or without legs crossed, arms folded or crossed behind the head) and you signal lack of interest, superiority or a failure to be convinced. Don't get paranoid about how you come across, but do check your body attitude and think what messages you might be giving.

– Many tutors are unnecessarily concerned about gestures and hand movements: 'I seem to wave my arms about a lot'. So do most people; it is the way that we emphasise a point, describe an object or action, and express emotion – just the things that a tutor needs to do when teaching. (There is a suggestion that human hand gestures are the vestigial remains of the sign language, which preceded the evolution of spoken language.) While you should avoid semaphoring and extreme mannerisms that the group will find distracting, make active use of hand and body gestures.

– Facial signals play an important part in human communications. A relatively large proportion of the brain is devoted to face recognition and the interpretation of facial gestures. We read reactions, emotions as well as intention in people's faces very quickly and the interpretations we make can take our overall understanding forward. Facial signals can belie a body message: leaning back, legs crossed with hands behind the head *but* with a genuine smile, eye contact and nodding says to someone 'Yes … good … tell me more'. Change to a sardonic smile and eyes to heaven and you are telling them something quite different! So actively use your face to communicate, and provide additional cues and clues to help people make sense of what you are saying and thinking.

5 Dress to suit the occasion and the audience as well as yourself. Some tutors wear occupational dress e.g. chef's whites, a painter's smock or exercise leotards: such rig indicates a professional approach to the topic though it needs to be carried off with panache. The unexpected can create attention and interest though painting your face with wode if you are a pre-medieval historian might be a step too far. Inappropriate clothing will detract from your credibility; think what you would expect a tutor to wear if you were a member of the group. Plan to look as if you have bothered about what you are wearing without being too formal or overly casual.

6 Though teaching is a professional activity, it is also one of human interaction and the rules of social communication apply just the same. When adult students describe the sort of tutor they like to work with, they talk about confidence, enthusiasm and friendliness. So whilst you should strive to appear self-assured, relaxed and quietly enthusiastic about your subject and your teaching, you should also smile, look friendly and act naturally since these signals say: 'I'm responsive ... I'm approachable ... I'm interested in your achievement and in you as a learning adult'.

KEY POINTS

- *Make positive use of your body language, social skills and personal attributes.*
- *Avoid behaviour that may distract people and get in the way of their learning.*

---

28 Difficult Students and Reluctant Attenders

It is not only new tutors who are worried about how to deal with difficult students; it is a perennial concern for most. Whilst problems can arise between individual students, a tutor and an adult group, they are seldom of the magnitude experienced by school teachers. Fortunately, discipline *per se* is rarely a problem; however, students can and do exhibit behaviours that need to be managed.

1   There are times when an individual's behaviour is perceived by a tutor as being difficult, where a closer look shows that it is the tutor's interpretation rather than a student's action that is the problem. It may be that you feel threatened because a student seems to be challenging your role within the group – or maybe questioning your knowledge base, your relative inexperience as a teacher, your lack of self-confidence, or your age relative to that of your students. It is less that an individual is difficult but rather that s/he provokes tutor insecurity. If this should happen to you, identify what tender spot is actually being tweaked and then decide how to cope with your feelings, rather than trying to modify a student's behaviour.

2   It is more likely, however, that the problem does have to do with the student. Its determinant(s) may be one or more of the following:

– a physical state	e.g. a disability; fatigue; illness
– a sense of difference	e.g. ethnicity; age; culture; gender
– a perceived disparity	e.g. knowledge; experience; qualification
– a failure to understand	e.g. too advanced; overly difficult
– a learning difficulty(s)	e.g. cognitive and/or affective
– a self perception	e.g. a lack of self-confidence
– a social apprehension	e.g. a sense of isolation; reactions to others

- a personality attribute   e.g. attention seeking; aggression
- a knowledge base   e.g. a know-it-all; 'monomaniac'
- an attitude   e.g. prejudice; discriminatory behaviour, including language and non verbal signals
- a behavioural response   e.g. overly talkative; overly quiet
- a requirement   e.g. compulsory attendance

3   There is no magic coping strategy though there are some principles and approaches that can help. The student *may* drop out or the offending behaviour may disappear but don't count on either! So:

- In the way you react:
    - do not be emotionally provoked
    - retain your self-control and dignity
    - diffuse any emotional heat within the group

- In your approach:
    - respect the student's adulthood and rights
    - look for the reason/source of the behaviour
    - allow the student to make his/her case if it seems appropriate

- In the manner in which you respond:
    - appeal to reason rather than emotion
    - avoid threats, sarcasm, ridicule and rudeness
    - avoid being patronising
    - avoid direct confrontation where you can … a quiet word is likely to be more effective
    - do, however, confront unacceptable discriminatory or prejudicial language and behaviour should it appear

- In what you say or do:
    - remind the student of any agreed ground rules
    - help the student recognise the needs of others in the group
    - offer to help the student in individual ways

- allow the student a face-saving option(s) or exit(s)
- use a tariff of controlling statements beginning at the gentlest

- If the group is *directly* involved:
  - ask other members for their feelings/responses
  - give them chance to moderate the deviance

- And later:
  - check that the student is content with the outcome
  - make an opportunity to talk through the experience, with a third party, especially about your residual feelings.

4 Whilst there is neither a stereotypical difficult student nor a universal solution, 'keeping your cool', treating people with respect, and using a tariff are particularly importance. Applied to an over-talkative student, a tariff might be:

- Thanks, Val, that's a fair point, what do other people think?
- Fine Val, but perhaps other people would like to add their views too
- Val, that's been a very complete opinion, but we would like to hear what others think as well
- Val, it really is important that we hear a representative range of views. As ever, you give us the benefit of your opinions but we do need to give everyone a chance so if you'd hold back …
- Val, hang on, please. We really must give every one the same chance to speak, and you're stopping others saying anything.

It is important that the group knows that you have recognised the problem even though you may be trying to avoid a show down. If your public tactics don't seem to be working, however, talk privately with the individual beyond the group's hearing. Offer confirmation of his/her good points as well as addressing the aberration, remembering it is the behaviour with which you are concerned, not the person.

5 If the behaviour is extreme and/or you feel it is beyond you, talk with your line manager. You do not and should not have to deal

with it on your own. There is nothing discreditable and everything professional in seeking help. The institution should have a student code of conduct, and a formal complaint/ grievance procedure in place. Find out what they say it will do and how it will do it. Be clear about your rights as a tutor as well as the rights of your students.

6   One far-reaching cause of problem behaviour is where attendance is mandatory. This may be a result of a vocational requirement or be part of a continued professional development programme. It could be a management 'remedy' for some individual's deficiency, though it is more likely to be a positive investment in that person to enhance and develop his/her skills further. However, when people are sent on courses inadequately briefed, they may fail to recognise it as a positive, confirming action, and decide that they have been found wanting in some way.

7   Reluctant attendance weighs heavily on the people concerned and can have a major impact on their motivation, cooperation and learning. A perception of training as an imposed remedy for inefficiency or ineffectiveness is only one of several determinants, however, and reluctance can also result from:

  – conflicting demands/activities
  – logistical problems
  – a lack of self-confidence in a course setting
  – antipathy to learning on a course and/or to a particular tutor
  – a fear of exposure through lack of knowledge/expertise
  – existing knowledge or experience being thought sufficient
  – a sense of superiority through rank, qualification or prior experience.

8   You might choose to ignore the dour looks and lack of enthusiasm, or you might offer people the choice of leaving though with a covert threat of likely consequences. These strategies are unlikely to encourage reluctant adults to modify their attitudes and join in should they stay. So:

- establish whether other people feel the same
- allow the group to air the issue(s) if the feeling is general
- offer to talk privately with an individual(s) if it is not.

Having once discovered why an individual(s) *is* a reluctant attender, some of the following may be useful:

- stress the concept of professional responsibility and the purpose(s) and benefits of ongoing learning/training
- draw parallels with comparable requirements/opportunities
- identify the potential benefits even for the more experienced and how others can benefit from what *s/he* knows
- point out possible/likely windfall gains
- promote the value of getting to know others and of networking
- show flexibility in what you plan to do, including a willingness to renegotiate some/all of the programme
- describe other related events and opportunities for progression to which the present session/event can lead
- make the course stimulating and relevant to everyone's needs.

9 Adults are responsible for themselves and for their actions, and reluctant attenders must make their own decisions to stay or leave. If they choose to stay, they may still 'withdraw' from the session, though if their behaviour distracts or impedes the group's learning and enjoyment, you must challenge it as being unacceptable. Assuming, however, that the positive choice has been made 'to make the best of being there', you should actively include them, acknowledging their interest and contributions though without overtly singling them out or being patronising. At the end, make an opportunity to speak with them, expressing your appreciation of their action(s) and confirming their contributions and achievements.

KEY POINTS

- *However you may be feeling inside, treat 'the problem student' with respect.*
- *Whilst you should try to respond to an individual's quirks and preferences, s/he is only one member of your group and you have a responsibility for everyone.*

---

29 Guidance, Progression and 'What Next?'

Adults have many reasons for wanting to learn more. The chapter on motivation discusses these in some detail though they can be categorised into those which have to do with job prospects and gaining qualifications, with further learning and creativity, with self-development and with social needs. ACL institutions will have some provision for student information and be able to link people to the local network of advisers and agencies who can offer further advice.

1 As a tutor, you aren't expected to offer detailed career guidance: providing information on education/training opportunities and jobs is the function of an Information, Advice and Guidance service, (IAG). Nevertheless, you are expected you to steer your students towards such provision, and more particularly, to acquaint them with the range of accessible opportunities to continue studying your particular area and other related subjects.

2 People can find help for major progression guidance in education at:

  - the Information, Advice and Guidance service (IAG)
  - Public libraries
  - Learndirect
  - Adult and community education centres and providers
  - Voluntary organisations and community centres
  - Open learning providers such as the Open University, Open College and the National Extension College
  - Private guidance agencies
  - Jobcentres
  - Special guidance projects for particular groups of people
  - Citizens Advise Bureaux (CABs).

3 Information about educational and training courses and other direct learning opportunities for adults can be found at:

- Adult Education Centres, Community Centres, some Sixth Form Colleges and some community schools
- UK online
- Learndirect
- Adult Residential Colleges
- Further Education and tertiary colleges (including Access courses)
- The University of the Third Age (U3A)
- The Women's Institute
- The Workers' Education Association (WEA)
- Universities and Institutes of Higher Education and their continuing education departments
- National societies and institutes
- Local clubs, societies, voluntary organisations, arts groups and leisure centres. Libraries and CABs usually have details
- Unitary authorities may also offer provision for particular subjects of local interest
- Basic Skills courses are held in local educational institutions.

Up-to-date addresses and websites of these and other national agencies and educational institutions are to be found in the current National Institute of Adult and Continuing Education (NIACE) Adult Learning Yearbook.

4   You can hardly avoid making some reference to 'what next' opportunities within your own subject as your teaching progresses; however, it is a good idea to put together a 'What Next' handout as a more complete *résumé* of such information. Give out a sheet listing the range of options for further study and other subject related activities/possibilities towards the end of the course and discuss it with the group. Keep it up to date ... and if you know that you are going to run another course(s), add it to the list!

   Include some/all of the following and give telephone numbers, addresses, contact names and www.sites where possible:

- local FE colleges; ACL centres; U3A; WEA; OU; university continuing education departments for day & week end

courses as well as sessional ones. Consult Learndirect
- local and national associations groups, clubs and societies and interest groups
- local/regional/national magazines and journals
- TV, film and radio programmes (Learning Zone)
- forthcoming live performances, films, festivals, shows and exhibitions
- books, videos, DVDs and CD ROMs
- specialist wholesale and retail outlets
- Internet sites – a rich source of material but they can also contain a lot of misinformation. Give specialist as well as general sites relating to your particular subject area
- libraries; archives; galleries; museums
- guided tours/walks/field trips
- possibilities for work as a volunteer or in paid employment.

KEY POINTS

- *Though all your students won't see your course as their route to mainstream educational provision or a job change, some might, so point them in the right direction.*
- *Offer people a range of opportunities to further their interest in your subject.*

---

30 Some Practical Points

If you still haven't had enough suggestions, here is a summary of the more practical!

- create a friendly, informal and welcoming atmosphere ... smile ... say 'Hello'!
- remember people's names and use them
- listen to what people say. It will help you find out more about them as learners and about their learning
- treat people as equals; adults resent being patronised and put down
- celebrate the diversity of people and personalities that come to your sessions, and provide for their variety of needs
- consult, and later negotiate with people about the course/sessions
- arrive early and don't rely on others to prepare things
- make the surroundings safe, attractive and congenial
- start and finish punctually; be first in and last out
- demonstrate an enthusiasm for your subject and for your teaching
- relate new material to what is already known, check that people understand and that they are learning
- use a variety of methods, especially participative ones, and change the activity frequently
- promote learning through active participation
- continually ask for, value and use people's experience and expertise
- use AVAs and resources to help learning
- offer students feedback, confirmation and constructive criticism on their work
- ensure that each individual leaves with a sense of having accomplished something and a desire to learn more
- remember that it is their learning that is important, not your teaching or your ego.
- if you don't enjoy teaching and working with adults, reconsider your position!

... and finally ...

Learning remains the responsibility of the learner; as teachers we cannot learn for our students. We can, however, strive to provide sound and accessible learning opportunities for them by thoughtful planning and preparation, which are designed to meet their needs, and by well run sessions, worthwhile assessment and feedback and careful evaluation of the whole process. Successful student achievement says something about the quality of our shared efforts: their adult learning and our adult teaching.

Further Reading

Here is a selection of texts in a growing market.

Teaching and Training in Post-compulsory Education
Andy Armitage, Robin Bryant et al., OUP, Second Edition, 2003.
    A thorough treatment with some practical guidance; for Level 4 Qualifications.

Adults Learning
    The monthly journal of NIACE, (National Institute of Adult and Continuing Education) and includes a variety of articles and up-to-date information on current developments in practice and policy plus news of forthcoming events. Worth subscribing to at NIACE, 19B, De Montfort Street, Leicester LE1 7GE; www.niace.org.uk

Teaching in Further Education
L.B. Curzon, Holt Education, 2003.
    A sound and well-revised text directed at FE teachers

Adult and Continuing Education
Peter Jarvis, Croom Helm, 1994 ... and ...

Adult Education and Lifelong Learning: Theory and Practice
Peter Jarvis, Routledge Farmer, 2003.
    Peter Jarvis is a veritable book factory; all his texts are good stuff.

Teaching Skills in Further and Adult Education
David Minton, Thomson Learning, 2005.
    Concentrates on FE rather than AE and slanted towards the Teachers' Certificate Course. Somewhat patchy.

NEC publications
    The National Extension College publishes a number of learning resources and training materials – especially useful on teacher development, counselling and guidance, open learning, basic

education, ESOL, etc. Rather pricey but get the brochure and see for yourself. (National Extension College, The Michael Young Centre, Purbeck Road, Cambridge, CB2 2HN; www.nec.ac.uk.)

NIACE publications
The NIACE produce a large range of well-written and accessible texts, which specifically targeted adult teaching and learning. These include: good practice; theories and ideas for practice; policy discussion; research; resources for teaching and training; and history and development of adult education. They are up-to-date and written by practitioners. Get the catalogue to see what they have in the areas of adult work that interests you – museum studies to adult literacy, and creative writing to ICT skills development. (NIACE, 19B, De Montfort Street, Leicester LE1 7GE; www.niace.org.uk

Journal of Adult and Continuing Education; Journal of Access Policy and Practice; Studies in the Education of Adults
All look at different aspects of post-initial education and training theory, practice and research. Rather academic. Look at library copies when you're feel strong. (NIACE, 19B, De Montfort Street, Leicester LE1 7GE www.niace.org.uk)

Teaching Adults
Alan Rogers, Open University Press, 2002.
Recommended. A thorough treatment, although idiosyncratic views. Particularly concerned with AE rather than FE. Valuable 'advanced companion' to *Adult Learning, Adult Teaching*.

Adult Learning
Jennifer Rogers, Open University Press, 2001.
One of the first and very readable. Lots of copies still around.

The Psychology of Adult Learning
Mark Tennant, Taylor and Francis, 1997.
The best text on this topic and a good reference source.

Look at **www.amazon.co.uk** and follow the link:
Education Studies and Teaching > Adult and Continuing Education.

INDEX

Index

Index